INDISPENSABLE

HOW TO SUCCEED AT YOUR FIRST JOB AND BEYOND

Quill

MEREDITH WHIPPLE CALLAHAN

Published by Inkshares, Inc., Oakland, California
www.inkshares.com

Cover design by Alban Fischer
Interior design by Kevin G. Summers

ISBN: 9781947848962
e-ISBN: 9781947848450
LCCN: 2018937932

First edition

Printed in the United States of America

CONTENTS

PREFACE

The idea for *Indispensable* came when I left my job at Bain & Company and prepared to attend Stanford Graduate School of Business. Taking my first break from work as a professional adult, I had time and space to reflect on the early years of my career. While I was proud of my strong performance and stellar reviews, I also knew that my success was not the result of my hard work alone. I had learned so much through both Bain's formal and informal training. I was also the lucky beneficiary of exceptional mentorship over the years. This got me thinking: what advice would I pass along to someone starting on the path I had just gone down? What had I learned that was universal and transferable?

I clawed back through the journals I kept during my early professional years and reflected upon what made me successful. I dug for insight from not only my own experiences but those of others. I conducted dozens of interviews with successful junior employees, managers of junior employees, and leaders in the talent space. I ran an online survey of over 175 employees to understand what made them and others successful in the workplace. Beyond this—and perhaps most importantly—I sat down with innumerable friends and colleagues who had been star performers in high-profile entry-level jobs, hashing out what advice they received and what they learned along the way. Finally, as the insights began to emerge, I collaborated with half a dozen talented MBAs and PhDs to check that the key points applied broadly, across industries. From my own experience and that of others, I started to pull together the essential puzzle pieces that would help employees to perform exceptionally.

The result was *Indispensable*. As you will see, this is not an academic tract on what makes employees successful. It is not the result of quantitative analysis or statistical proofs, nor is it a redaction of other workplace advice. Instead, *Indispensable* is a synthesis of real-life experiences in some of the most prestigious and challenging entry-level jobs out there.

I wish you the best in your work life, and I hope you find *Indispensable* useful. For those of you starting your careers, the advice here is meant to accelerate you along your path. For those of you later in your careers, I hope this prompts you to reflect on what made you successful along the way—whether it was by these strategies or others—and to emerge better equipped to mentor the next generation of employees.

For more information or to engage further in the *Indispensable* conversation, visit my website, www.indispensablebook.com. I appreciate your input and know that it will help make the next edition of this book even broader and richer.

Meredith Whipple Callahan
Norwalk, CT

Note: As you read *Indispensable*, you will see that I alternate the gender of the managers and employees in each chapter. For example, chapter 1 refers to all managers as male and all other employees as female, while chapter 2 refers to all managers as female and all other employees as male. While this stark gender divide is obviously unrealistic, the alternating approach helps avoid gender bias around roles so as to be more consciously inclusive.

INTRODUCTION

You are not the typical employee. You are not satisfied by merely eking out an existence. You refuse to execute your tasks mindlessly. You cannot get excited about hurrying through the week as you wait for the weekend.

No, you have higher ambitions and better prospects. You want to be challenged and engaged. You want to excel at your job. In addition to promotions, raises, and the corner office (or whatever indicates success in your chosen field), you want respect, autonomy, and satisfaction. In short, you want to prove that you are so talented, so effective, and so helpful that you are considered *indispensable* by your organization. But how to begin? Work long hours? Cross all your t's and dot all your i's? Buy the boss a muffin basket?

Indispensable: How to Succeed at Your First Job and Beyond provides direction for becoming the best employee you can be. Whether you're starting a new job, meeting a new manager, or taking on a new assignment, *Indispensable* gives you the strategies you need to excel. Over twelve chapters, this book outlines the characteristics of indispensable employees and gives practical solutions for developing each skill.

Why You Should Care

What is meaningful about becoming indispensable? Why is it worth the effort? The benefits of indispensability include more security in your current role, greater satisfaction and fulfillment in the workplace, and better professional opportunities in the future.

The most basic benefit of becoming indispensable is exactly that: indispensability. When the economy takes a dive, pink slips materialize and long-term job security disappears. In tough times, distinguishing yourself from the pack helps preserve your paycheck. Becoming indispensable also helps prevent underemployment, a state in which you may settle for a job that demands less than you are able to contribute. As an indispensable employee, you are more likely to have and keep the job that fits your skills and ambitions.

That said, the intangible benefits of indispensability are even more rewarding; not only do indispensable employees have jobs, but they are also more likely to enjoy their jobs. Smart organizations know that employees seek engagement at the highest level; workers want a sense of purpose, the opportunity to contribute, inclusion in a community, and the support to learn and develop. Indispensable employees are more likely to realize all these aspirations. You are given more interesting and important work. You are entrusted to tackle that work autonomously, minimizing the need for close management. Ultimately, as an indispensable employee, you are more likely to be not just satisfied with your job but delighted by it.

It is shortsighted to count the benefits of indispensability to your current situation alone. Ultimately, indispensability pays off with the opportunity to learn and grow in both this role and the next. Becoming indispensable allows you to accelerate your career path and, more importantly, to accelerate your professional growth. Positive performance assessments give indispensable employees leverage to secure plum new projects, and satisfied managers are more likely to suggest indispensable employees for promotions. And, while they may not be able to imagine life without them, managers are also more likely to provide positive references for indispensable employees when they move on to another organization. Thus, though *Indispensable* may appear to be about becoming indispensable to one manager, the book helps you become indispensable along your entire career path, reaping the tangible and intangible benefits along the way.

How This Book Is Organized

Despite the great variety of jobs out there, the qualifications many companies tend to look for in their junior employees are remarkably similar. Most professional jobs require a similar set of essential skills focused around organization, problem solving, communication, and teamwork. Thus, whether you are designing furniture or balancing the books, a common set of strategies will help you become excellent.

Indispensable is split into three sections that cover this suite of skills: Nail the Basics, Excel at Execution, and Exceed Expectations. These sections are broadly organized to build in both chronology (from skills you can demonstrate at the beginning to those you can show later) and complexity (from simpler skills to more complex skills).

First, you **nail the basics**. These are the underlying requirements for not only becoming an indispensable employee but being a functional worker. Toward this end, you present yourself professionally, adopt a great attitude, and invest yourself in the mission of your organization. You also seek out information about your position, organization, and industry, understanding this information will be useful as you progress. You are thoughtful about starting strong and setting yourself up for long-term success. Remembering that reputations are set early and become hard to change, you demonstrate these indispensable traits from day one. Chapters 1–4 help you lay that foundation.

Second, you **excel at execution**. As you tackle your work, you take pains to execute even the least interesting of tasks in an efficient and error-free manner. You know that reliability is a prerequisite for more responsibility. Then, as you gain experience, you execute your job better and better. You finish your work well and communicate effectively. You bravely address problems and tackle interpersonal issues. Task by task, you prove yourself, building confidence and earning trust. Chapters 5–9 help you prove your competence and excel at the tasks within your scope.

Finally, you **exceed expectations.** As an indispensable employee, you do more than is asked of you. Instead of sticking to your narrow job description, you make an impact beyond those particular responsibilities. You stretch to take on more responsibility. You take the initiative to improve your organization broadly. You also proactively push your own professional development, going beyond the formal feedback processes to drive your growth. Chapters 10–12 lay out strategies for going beyond excellent execution and exceeding all expectations. This is the realm of becoming fully indispensable; here you lay the groundwork to advance from an indispensable employee to a manager and leader of others.

How to Use This Book

Each chapter of *Indispensable* focuses on one aspect of work and proposes four or five essential strategies for doing that well. Each of these strategies also includes a set of "Indispensable

Solutions," practical suggestions that help you apply that strategy more tangibly. Collectively, this means that there are more than fifty strategies of becoming indispensable.

Given this number of strategies, you may wonder where to start and how to prioritize your time. It is important to know that no single strategy is more important than the others. While you need not display every quality all of the time, indispensability comes from bringing a strong suite of skills to your organization. To get the most out of *Indispensable*, read through all the strategies and consider how each one applies to you. The more dimensions of yourself you can develop, the more likely you are to be indispensable and to find the satisfaction that comes with that.

That said, a subset of these strategies is likely to be most relevant to your current role at this moment in time. Jobs are different; developing a marketing campaign for Coca-Cola in Pondicherry is unlike designing apps in Denver. Similarly, bosses are different; one looks for concise communication while another wants to ensure that you cover all the details. Though you develop yourself broadly (for this job and the next), you may want to focus on only a couple of strategies today. Think critically about what handful of strategies is most pertinent at this moment—to both your current situation and your personal development.

As you progress, you will also apply the indispensable strategies in a way that is more and more consistent with your unique style and personality. For example, while some of the conflict-management approaches would sound very natural coming from one person, they could seem insincere when used by another (see chapter 9, "Take On Conflict Productively"). Similarly, different employees may find themselves endorsing the mission of their organization in different ways; one employee may wear the company's motto on her sleeve, while another may quietly but sincerely ascribe to its values (see chapter 3, "Invest Yourself in the Mission"). The indispensable strategies are yours to use. Do not subsume yourself and your unique personality to these strategies; endeavor to make them yours over time.

Of course, all of this will take work. You cannot passively read this book and reap the benefits. This does not necessarily mean you work longer hours than others, but you will apply yourself more intentionally than those around you. You will approach your work in a more thoughtful way, considering what you are doing and why. You will dedicate yourself to not only the tasks of your job but also to the self-development work that accompanies personal growth. As you likely already guessed, there are no tips, tricks, or shortcuts to excelling at your job. Instead, becoming indispensable requires the development of skills over time. Though you may have to focus your development on only a handful of strategies at a time, you will eventually build a portfolio of ways that you are indispensable. To get the most out of *Indispensable*, you need to commit to making that investment.

Remember: You are not the typical employee. You have higher aspirations. And now you have in your hand the practical playbook for becoming excellent at your job, happier in your workplace, and indispensable to your organization. By opening this book and beginning the journey, you are already on track to becoming your best self at work. Enjoy the journey toward becoming indispensable.

NAIL THE BASICS

Becoming indispensable is like building a tower: you need to set a solid foundation before reaching higher heights. This foundation may feel basic—just poured concrete with none of the shiny glass panes or fancy fixtures—but it is essential. The foundation is required to hold up everything from the first steel beams to the final finishes.

Chapters 1–4 cover the foundations you need. You will learn to give yourself every advantage as you show up on time, come prepared, and demonstrate that you care. You will understand what it means to have a winning attitude, bringing a combination of humility, enthusiasm, kindness, and team spirit to your responsibilities. You will reflect on what it looks like to invest yourself in the mission, aligning your purpose to the demands of your job and the goals of your organization. Finally, you will become actively curious in a way that is rare among employees, taking it upon yourself to learn everything you can about your role, organization, and industry from the outset. So, put on your overalls, pick up your trowel, and get ready to pour some solid foundations.

CHAPTER ONE

Show Up and Start Strong

Like it or not, books are often judged by their covers. Trashy romance novels featuring sweaty couples convey one impression. Sober textbooks stamped with pointed titles like *Fluid Dynamics* and *Particle Physics* convey another.

From day one on the job, you will be judged by everything external. Do you present yourself professionally? Do you care enough to follow directions? Are you prepared? Do you seem engaged and interested? As soon as you walk in the door, your colleagues will start forming opinions from how you present yourself.

Happily, this presentation is easily managed to your best advantage. Employees working on becoming indispensable ensure their appearance and actions give the consistent impression that they are useful contributors to their organizations. They manage the little things—the time they show up, the way they sit, and the materials they bring—to create positive first impressions.

Though you may fritter away your first month on the job finding the bathroom, deciphering the org chart, and waiting for someone to tell you what to do, you can still give a good impression while you are doing it. The following strategies will help you to show up and start strong.

1) Be There When They Need You

If you want to move up in the world, you cannot live and die by the clock, anxiously awaiting five o'clock and freedom. There are very few executives who log off as they leave the office and expect to be free until morning. The most important contributors in any organization are the people who are willing to be there when they are needed, whenever that may be.

At first, it will be obvious when you are needed; you will be told something easy to interpret, like "Our day starts at 9:00 a.m." or "The production meeting is at 2:30 p.m." Thus, the first rule of being there when they need you is showing up when they explicitly tell you to be there. Arrive promptly. Be visibly at your desk when you are supposed to be there. And be on time—or better, slightly early—for meetings.

Beyond this, you will need to use judgment to determine the times when you are most needed. Is it most important that you be at your desk at 10:35 a.m. when the lumber orders come in? Or is it more important that you pull down daily stock price information right after the markets close? In addition to the specific times you are asked to be present, there will be certain windows in your day when you are needed—right here, right now. Identify these important periods in the flow of your job and be willing to manage your snack and coffee breaks around them.

Of course, the most important time to be available is exactly when your colleagues are looking for you. Your manager's schedule may not be entirely predictable; he may have a different lineup of meetings every day. This might make it impossible for you to predict when he is expecting you to be around. But even if you are not always waiting at your desk, you are always responsive to your manager's call. If he calls you during lunch with an emergency, you are available to sort it out. If there is last-minute work to be done on a Sunday night, you can take care of it. Responsiveness does not mean being chained to your desk, becoming a slave to your phone, or ending your social life, but it does mean being available when needed. There will be time later to strike the right balance between work and life, but, particularly as you start out, you should be there when they need you.

Indispensable Solutions

- Have an open conversation with your manager on expectations around work hours and availability. Like many things, simply discussing the topic up front goes a long way toward avoiding issues later.

- If being physically present matters to your company (i.e., if there is an expectation of face time), be savvy to the dynamics. Sometimes this is a matter of putting in enough hours. Other times, it is a matter of putting in the *right* hours. For example, colleagues may penalize someone who gets in after they do in the morning, even if the same person stays much later at night.

- While you are present at work, make sure that each minute in your seat is as productive as possible. This means being focused and effective while you are required to be in the office, so that by the time you are allowed to punch out, you can do so quickly and confidently. (See chapter 6, strategy 2, "Pump Up Productivity," for more ideas.)

- Just as there are times when you are needed, so are there times when you are not needed. Loitering around the office because you feel like you should be there (when you are clearly doing nothing) is not good for you. If face time is a reality, figure out how to make yourself productive otherwise. If face time is not a concern, take a break and leave the office during working hours. Using excess professional time wisely also gives you the flexibility to be available on personal time if necessary.

- Make technology work for you. Though your phone may keep you tethered to work during evenings and weekends, it can also free you at other times. Take every advantage of connectivity technology. Many times, you need not be tied to your desk to be highly responsive.

- Figure out the expectations around response times for the different mediums of communication at your job. Are you expected to respond to emails immediately, within a day, or within a week? Similarly, how quickly are you supposed to return voice mails, telephone calls, or texts? Ensure that you do not get branded as lazy simply because you do not have the same expectations on timelines as others around you.

- Be smart on lifestyle trade-offs. If you know that there is a big deadline coming up on Wednesday and that late nights are a possibility, do not buy tickets for the Red Sox game on Tuesday. Do not set yourself up to make a reluctant sacrifice and resent your team. You can always pick up a couple of bleacher seats at the last minute if you do not have to stay late.

- If possible, get visibility into your manager's calendar. Looking a couple of days out into the future, you are able to see when meetings are happening and predict your own deliverables accordingly. Even better, you may be able to help your manager prepare for the meeting with the CEO he has not even started considering.

- Respect your supervisor's time. The flip side of being accessible to your manager is understanding that your manager is not always accessible to you. Show that you do not take his time for granted. When possible, ask questions like "Is now still a good time?" and "Do you have a minute?" to give your manager the option of choosing when to engage, rather than forcibly making yourself the center of his universe.

2) Dress the Part (or Not)

Following certain dress codes in the workplace—closed-toed shoes, laboratory goggles, or surgical masks—can be important to protecting your health and safety. Following other dress codes—say, knee-length skirts, collared shirts, or jackets—may seem less relevant to performing well. In both cases, however, others may consider your appearance as a visible sign that you are mature, ready for the workplace, and soon-to-be indispensable.

For some of us, it is easy to conform to whatever dress code is expected. We simply adjust our presentation—clothes, shoes, hair, and otherwise—to meet expectations. We harness these external cues to show that we are ready to integrate into the culture of the organization and be effective at our jobs.

For others of us, this may be more difficult. Our appearance is often intertwined with important dimensions of our identity—precious parts of ourselves that we want to wear on the outside. If you are a person who invests your identity in your appearance, you may feel challenged by dressing as your organization expects. Your pink hair, combat boots, or three-piece suit may be a key building block of your identity, and abandoning it for work may feel like a betrayal of yourself.

In this case, assess the culture carefully. Is this a place where you can be your full self? Or is this a place that will judge you for your appearance? You may argue that dressing the part is irrelevant to your performance. You may contend that any intelligent boss will see through your appearance to uncover your talents. Yes. Perhaps. But for every wise boss you are lucky enough to work for, there are three, thirty, or three hundred and thirty others who will be happy to judge you by your cover rather than the good work you will do.

This is the realm in which others' opinions may force you to make hard trade-offs between being who you are and look- ing as they would expect. There is no right answer on how to navigate these waters. The key is being able to make a con- scious, eyes-wide-open decision about the path you choose and the risk you may take. By doing so, even if you do not look as they would expect, you display your thoughtful consideration and underlying principles—building blocks of indispensability.

Indispensable Solutions

- Tailor your appearance to the different contexts in which you work. While you might be able to get away with jeans in the office, you may need to dust off your interview suit for a client meeting (or vice versa). Dressing the part often requires subtle fine-tuning to the events of the day rather than just adhering to a dress code.

- Consider not only how you dress to fit in but also how you dress to stand out. What is your go-to outfit that makes you feel powerful, positive, and put together? The "power suit" phenomenon is real. Figure out your go-to outfit for the days that you need the extra support.

- Organize your closet to support your ambitions. Separating your work clothes from the rest of your wardrobe can save time and energy on a draggy Monday morning. It may also save you from accidentally donning those loafers that might be a bit too scuffed for your high-stakes meeting.

- Pick out your clothes the night before. The act of choosing something appropriate will force you to check your calendar and mentally prepare in advance.

- Do not become so attached to your wardrobe staples that you wear them down and wear them out. While you might think those pants look as lovely as they did the day you bought them, a pair of fresh eyes can see that they are getting a bit worn. Holes in linings or pockets indicate that, however well that item of clothing has served you, it is time to love it and let it go.

3) Bring the Right Tools for the Job

When headed to work, be a Boy Scout. No, you do not need to bring your compass and waterproof matches to work. Instead, adopt the Boy Scout motto of "Be prepared." Always take time before starting the task at hand to think about what tools and materials you will need to get the job done. Maybe this includes a laptop. Maybe a calculator. Maybe even your old scouting handbook. Whatever they may be, make sure that you bring the right tools for the job.

Remember that preparation is not only physical; it is mental as well. Perhaps you do not need to take anything in particular to a meeting, but you should be able to speak fluently on your project's status. Think about the overall agenda and what your role will be in the meeting: Are you going to be leading an interview? Reporting on your department's budget? Contributing ideas for a new marketing plan? Be prepared with facts and figures, opinions and observations to complete your role to the best of your ability.

While bringing the things you need, also be careful to leave behind the things you do not need. Who is going to call you on your cell phone during your one-on-one meeting with your manager? How will it look to be eating your yogurt in the middle of the team update? Is it appropriate to bring your dog to this meeting, regardless of the pet-friendly policy? The answers to these questions will depend on your company culture; the indispensable employee brings only that which projects engagement, readiness, and focus, and leaves the rest behind.

In the end, bringing the right tools for the job is just another way of indicating that you are engaged in your work, thoughtful about the task at hand, and ready to attack your responsibilities.

Indispensable Solutions

- If the physical things you need for your job are consistent from day to day, make a checklist you can consult. Items you may need for working in an office environment include a pen or pencil, paper or a notebook, a laptop, a projector, a remote mouse, print-outs of your work (for yourself, for others), additional visual aids, print-outs of backup or supporting work, whiteboard markers, Post-it notes, and business cards.

- Approach your meetings like you approached your job interview. Before interviewing, you considered what questions they might ask and prepared your response for each. Similarly, before going to a meeting, think about what questions you could be asked and what answers you will give. Then make sure you have all the information you need to answer those questions effectively. Do not hesitate to write your thoughts down to reference during the meeting.

- For double bonus points, reflect on what your manager needs as well. This is an especially good approach when you are struggling to figure out how to contribute as the low man on the totem pole. You may not have made the PowerPoint presentation, but you do have the projector and remote mouse. This is not the be-all and end-all of contributing to your organization, but it is certainly a start. By being prepared with what he will need, your manager gets accustomed to seeing you as useful from the outset.

- When in doubt, bring a pen and paper. Showing up empty-handed does not leave a good impression.

4) Look Like You Care (Because You Do)

You are out at your local dive bar and, even though you cannot hear a thing over the music, you can easily figure out what is going on: that sly smile, a particular tone of voice, a certain lean into a conversation.

The cues as to what is going on in the workplace on Monday morning are just as strong as they are in the bar on Saturday night. Your body language announces to your colleagues exactly how you feel about them, this interesting brainstorming session, or that ridiculous new policy for the coffee machine. An indispensable employee uses body language that conveys her interest, her competence, and her value. She is careful to not undermine herself with physical indicators of laziness, disinterest, or impatience.

Body language is not just how you sit in your chair. It is your posture, your gestures, your facial expressions, and even your degree of eye contact. Be aware of how you present yourself along each of these dimensions. It takes attention, but once you remember to tune into your body, managing your body language will become easier.

Indications that you care include (and are interpreted as) the following.

- Sitting up straight: "I am present. I am ready."

- Leaning into a conversation: "I am listening to what you are saying."

- Nodding: "I agree with you."

- Taking notes: "What you are saying is worthwhile. It is important for me to remember."

- Making eye contact: "I am a confident contributor. Go ahead, try me."

On the other hand, the following postures signal a disengagement that may undermine credibility. These mannerisms may stem from boredom, annoyance, or needing to go to the bathroom, but they do not give the impression that you care.

- Texting on your phone during a meeting: "I have many better things to do than be here—like checking the weather in Albuquerque." (If you are awaiting communication—such as an important business message or a call regarding a family situation—it may make sense to inform the others in the meeting in advance.)

- Not taking notes (especially when taking instructions): "To your great annoyance, I will promptly forget everything you said and make you repeat it later."

- Crossing your arms in front of your chest: "Whether I will admit it or not, I disagree."

- Fiddling: "I am nervous and uncomfortable, or I have to go to the bathroom."

- Rocking in your chair: "I have the attention span of a four-year-old."

- Putting your feet on your desk: "I am in charge." (But you probably are not.)

- Rolling eyes: "How stupid do you think I am?"

- Avoiding eye contact: "I have no clue what I am doing and am trying to hide that from you."

────────────── **Indispensable Solutions** ──────────────

- While it is easy to look alert and engaged for the first fifteen minutes of an hour-long meeting, the following forty-five minutes can seem interminable. Over this time, your posture may slowly disintegrate, Frosty the Snowman style: you may slouch a bit more, your head may hang a bit lower, and your shoulders may start to droop. In marathon meetings, set mid-meeting reminders to check your posture and look alive; pick a place in the agenda, a time on the clock, or anything else to prompt you to check in mentally and physically.

- In addition to diagnosing your body language, assess your nervous habits. Do you have a problem with biting your nails? With wringing your hands? With sniffling or sneezing? Do a quick assessment (either independently or by asking a friend) in order to figure out your (often unconscious) nervous tendencies and work on eliminating them.

- Taking notes is a universally recognized indicator that something important is being said. Given this, do yourself a favor and take notes. Regardless of how smart you are, how simple the instructions are, or how unimportant the task may seem: write it down, write it down, write it down. This is particularly true when your supervisor is speaking, when someone is giving instructions, and, above all else, at the intersection of these two: when your supervisor is giving you instructions.

- The best way to look like you care in a meeting is to participate. Unless you are invited as an observer, try to speak up within the first quarter of any meeting you are invited to join (often the first ten to fifteen minutes of an hour-long meeting). If possible, it is helpful if your contribution is a statement and not a question, though any involvement is positive.

5) Follow Basic Instructions

At the top of every test in elementary school, there was a short paragraph of instructions. It gave basic guidance: Use a number two pencil. Do not go outside the lines. Write your name on the top of every page of the test. Though these instructions seemed obvious, failing to follow them meant losing significant points.

Similarly, the first things you will be asked to do at work may seem basic. You will have to fill out forty-five forms for human resources. You will be tasked with reading the entire employee manual. Or you will sit through hours of e-learning modules on compliance. Whatever the task, you may be tempted to gloss over the entire exercise and move through it quickly.

However simple the task, as an indispensable employee, you remember what you learned in kindergarten: especially on the simple stuff, you pay attention, apply yourself, and follow the instructions. Give yourself the highest likelihood of getting an A.

Indispensable Solutions

- Always complete standard administrative tasks correctly and properly, well before they are due. Do not make your manager follow up to see if you completed that mess of legal paperwork yet. Failing to follow through on basic tasks not specific to your role undermines your manager's faith in your ability to execute more complete tasks requiring specialized knowledge.

- As you begin a new role, be sure to follow the instructions given instead of inventing your own. While your ideas for change may be far better than the status quo, follow your employer's way of doing things first so you can learn the existing ways of working.

- It is tempting to want to move on to complex tasks quickly in order to prove yourself in a new role. Do not be afraid of starting small and starting simple. Following instructions on basic tasks helps lay the foundation to take on more in the future.

CHAPTER TWO

Adopt a Winning Attitude

Though attitude is not everything, it is far from nothing. Organizations want employees who are not only good at their jobs, but who adopt a winning attitude as well. These employees approach their jobs with enthusiasm, regardless of the task. They balance confidence in themselves with an appropriate humility and respect for others. They are polite and kind, the type of people who see their colleagues as human beings who are worth knowing. When faced with a challenge, they work collaboratively and constructively with their teammates.

More so than any other aspect of your job, your attitude is under your control. By simply changing your attitude, you can determine whether work will be fun or a total drag. You can whine your way through the crappy jobs or dispatch undesirable tasks quickly and efficiently. You can choose to smile, or you can choose to frown. And, however clichéd it may seem, by changing from one to the other, you can turn your entire perspective on work upside down.

So, forget being an employee whom others want to have on their team. Indispensable employees are, even more importantly, the type of people that others want to be around both inside and outside of work.

1) Start with Humility

In his autobiography, Ben Franklin aspires to develop his humility. His mantra: "Imitate Jesus and Socrates." While you need not agree with his choice of paragons, new employees should share the same goal. Too often, whether they are coming from a lifetime of scholastic achievement or a vaunted position at another company, new hires can overestimate their abilities and turn off their colleagues. There is nothing more ridiculous to a seasoned veteran than watching yet another novice swagger into the office, boasting about new ideas before understanding the context. This kind of bragging is reminiscent of those bombastic infomercials: "He slices! He dices! He balances the budget!" Is there anything he cannot do?

Even though you will accomplish unprecedented achievements, do not alienate your coworkers by turning them off on day one. As they say at Haas Graduate School of Business, project "confidence without attitude." Let your achievements speak for themselves, and your colleagues will support you rather than resent you from the outset. And in the meantime, you certainly have a lot to learn from all of them.

--- **Indispensable Solutions** ---

- Remember that you do not know what you do not know. Though you may think that you understand the context of a situation, you cannot be sure. Tread lightly at the beginning and seek first to understand.

- Know that when you present yourself as God's gift to your organization, managers have ways of showing you just how much there is to learn. They can give you assignments that you cannot possibly succeed at, just to take you down a notch.

- Show that you respect not only your superiors but also others who are more tenured within your organization. This includes everyone from the CEO's assistant to the head of housekeeping. Everyone has something to teach you; some of the wisest people in your organization may not be the best credentialed or the most senior. As you start out, ask anyone and everyone for advice. Over time, maintain respect.

- To help you avoid the temptation of resting on your laurels, keep your self-congratulatory paraphernalia at home. That goes for everything from fancy university diplomas in Latin to old Little League trophies.

- Though arrogance is to be avoided, a healthy dose of confidence is still necessary to become indispensable. While recognizing what you must learn, you should be simultaneously confident that you can learn it. Indeed, you will master it. It will just take time and hard work. As you move forward, you can increasingly pair your novice humility with a modest confidence.

2) Approach Every Task with Enthusiasm

Employees—particularly young, well-educated, and historically successful new hires—often have a hard time doing the grunt work. They balk at being asked to fetch coffee, make photocopies, or set up a room for a meeting. But it turns out that even the loftiest of CEOs have to worry about recording their voicemail greetings just right. Even the best of lawyers have to print copies of briefs when their assistants go on vacation to the Poconos. And even the President of the United States has to decide what pen to use when signing executive orders.

It is unfortunate, but true: regardless of how sexily the HR coordinator described your job, not every task at work is challenging, interesting, and intellectually engaging. As a new hire, you cannot be too good for the uninspiring tasks. And even as an experienced employee, you still are not too good for them. Colleagues respect employees who are willing to roll up their sleeves and pitch in—regardless of their tenure in the organization.

Indispensable Solutions

- Do the annoying tasks in a timely manner. It may be tempting to put them off for another day, but doing them right away minimizes the pain.

- If you are inclined to reticence, introversion, or skepticism, you need not cake on a false layer of bubbly, extroverted enthusiasm to be effective. Your underlying willingness to take on the task at hand—not the number of high fives you give along the way—is what really matters.

- Regardless of your personality, do not complain about menial tasks. You do not need to proclaim how much you love to format PowerPoint slides when you really do not, but outright complaining is off-limits. It undermines the goodwill you built for doing the work in the first place.

• For whatever you might find yourself tasked with, there is likely something worse that you could be doing. Content yourself with your lot in life by imagining how much worse it could all be: you could be a shark suit tester, a snake wrangler, or a cranberry bog farmer. Worse, you could be unemployed.

• Though it is good to be responsive to your manager, beware of being so conciliatory that you get stepped on more than the office doormat. It is one thing to be the team player who pitches in when the department is in a crunch. It is quite another thing to be the sucker who ends up being the only person in the office making photocopies on a Saturday for the twenty-fourth time.

3) Just Be Nice

While you learned to follow basic instructions in kindergarten (see chapter 1, strategy 5, "Follow Basic Instructions"), you learned how to be nice in preschool. With any luck, you performed well on the "Plays Well with Others" dimension on your report cards, earning a bounty of gold stars and scratch-and-sniff stickers. In that case, being nice to others should not be a problem. On the other hand, if you often got demerits for stealing blocks, spitting milk at your tablemates, or hogging the mat during nap time, this strategy is for you. Remember the basic dos and don'ts of kindness.

Being nice starts with simple politeness and expressing sincere interest in others as human beings. To this end, make sure that you do the following:

• Introduce yourself. Everyone is worth knowing, period. Introductions are typically awkward for both parties, so swallow your discomfort and initiate the engagement instead of waiting for the other person to do it first.

- If you recall nothing else, remember names. If necessary, use one of the many silly mnemonic devices available to help you do so (see a list of tactics in the Indispensable Solutions section at the end of this strategy).

- Beyond names, remembering a couple of personal details goes a long way toward making a connection. Did she get married last year? Do his kids love pasta? Does she hate Tom Hanks movies? Given the technology available, there is no excuse for not making notes somewhere (in your contacts, in a text file) to help you remember those details. That said, mention only the things that have come up between you in person; information you found online is a creepy conversation starter.

- Be sincerely interested in getting to know people on a meaningful level. Try to go beyond platitudes about the weather and the weekend. Ask open-ended questions and follow these up with next-level inquiries. Turn on your curiosity.

- Smile. Psychologists claim that it makes you happier, and it certainly makes you more approachable.

- Be patient.

- Treat others with respect. You will not receive what you do not afford to others.

- Default to being inclusive instead of exclusive. Invite others to events that you plan rather than needlessly hurting feelings.

On the other hand, do not shoot yourself in the foot by being impolite—or worse, by being actively mean. Ensure you follow these guidelines:

- Do not let common courtesies fall by the wayside. Put your finishing school training to good use and remember to say hello, goodbye, please, and thank you. Thank-you notes in particular, whether via email or on paper, are a powerful and underutilized tool in the workplace.

- Do not speak out in anger. Instead, pause and breathe. Then flip to chapter 9, strategy 3, "Balance Directness and Diplomacy," to approach the situation in a useful way instead of saying something you will soon regret.

- Do not insert yourself into office politics. Particularly, do not take sides in conflicts that do not involve you. This may involve leaving the room to avoid association.

- Do not burn bridges. Organizations, industries, and, ultimately, the world are all smaller than you think.

Indispensable Solutions

- Take pains to meet everyone you can during your first days and weeks on the job. Introduce yourself. Put names to faces and faces to names immediately rather than associating with only your new clique of work besties.

- Remember: However unimportant, incomprehensible, or evil your coworker may seem to be, everyone is a human being. They were born a helpless baby. They will become a tottering senior. They may have a spouse and kids at home, or at least a dog, cat, or goldfish. On some level, they are just like you. They are human, they are vulnerable, and they are loved by someone on this planet. Do not write them off.

- Here is the list of aforementioned shortcuts to remembering names:

  - Upon first hearing the name, repeat it silently to yourself a couple of times to cement it in your memory.

  - Note the physical features of the person before you. Does she have a distinctive nose? Does he wear great neckties? Does she have a celebrity doppelgänger? Associate that obvious feature or resemblance (which you are bound to recognize next time) with their name. Think, *Christine looks a lot like Emma Stone.*

  - Use the name right away in conversation ("As Yumiko was just saying . . ."). Use it when leaving as well ("Nice to meet you, Yumiko").

  - Rebound in the first interaction. If you forget their name as soon as they mention it, do not hesitate to ask again immediately ("I'm sorry, what is your name again?"). Recovering early on is easily forgiven, while asking their name again on your third meeting is nothing but awkward.

4) Collaborate Rather Than Compete

There are all sorts of words for people who focus more on themselves than the collective: Loners. Divas. Recluses. Though some of them may be lauded for their genius, even the most talented of these are admired with qualifiers: "He is a great programmer but a notoriously bad teammate." "She is a great engineer but makes the marketing and sales teams miserable." "He is such a good analyst but refuses to let anyone else touch his Excel models."

However talented you may be, you could not run the show by yourself if you tried. You could not set the strategy, develop the product, design the packaging, find the distributors, manage the ad campaign, balance the books, and administer the payroll and benefits, all while running twenty-three manufacturing plants. No, in addition to being too much work for one person, you are unqualified to do all of it well. Thank goodness you play for a team.

Even if you are in an individual contributor role, you still need to succeed as part of the broader organization. In collaborating, you figure out how you can best achieve your mission together. In competing, you focus more on how you look compared to others. Focus your energies on the first approach. Understand that you do not need to have the best answer or be the smartest person in the room to be a useful contributor. Instead, without getting caught up in comparisons, recognize that you can play your own unique role in contributing to the team's success.

Indispensable Solutions

- Remember that your team is not only your cubiclemates, your working group, or your department. Your team consists of your entire organization—from finance to human resources, from interns to executives.

- Competition can fuel motivation, but it rarely results in fully positive outcomes. Colleagues whom you have "beaten" will not be eager to work with you or for you, but may rather resent you. Teamwork is about working together to win the game. If you injure or undermine a teammate, you only weaken your chances of ultimate success.

- As a member of the team, you do not scramble over your colleagues to get to the finish line first. Instead, even when performing well yourself, seek to raise the level of the whole team. You would rather be Everest, the highest peak in the massive Himalayan range, than the tallest little molehill in Death Valley.

CHAPTER THREE

Invest Yourself in the Mission

At the outset of *Mission: Impossible*, the mission commander always delivered the same signature line: "Your mission, should you choose to accept it . . ." This was followed by some exotic assignment—recover a stolen item, save the hostages, or stop a deadly virus from spreading. As an employee, you have been similarly entrusted with a mission. Your job is perhaps not as high-stakes as sneaking into vaults and rappelling down buildings, but it is your mission nevertheless.

Indispensable employees choose to accept their organization's mission and invest themselves in its attainment. They connect the day-to-day of what they do to the company's broader mission. They also connect the company's mission to their personal purpose. This connection is not superficial or forced; they find the natural alignment between the organization's objectives and their own direction.

1) Align Work to Your Personal Purpose

Indispensable is not a book about finding your purpose in life. It is not about discovering your love of derivatives trading during your ride on the Trans-Siberian Railway. It is not about figuring out if you should leave your job as a call center worker in Bangalore to become an IT consultant in Pune. While souls, searching, and soul-searching are all important, they are not the focus here. Instead, this book focuses on making you indispensable within the context of whatever job you choose to do.

That said, you should choose wisely. First, invest the time to get to know yourself. Do not be deterred if you lack clarity on your life's purpose. For many, insight into your purpose comes piecemeal over time. You get glimpses here and there of what lights you up. It often takes an accumulation of both experience and reflection to see your purpose more clearly.

With whatever insight you do have, choose a job that is well aligned to your life purpose as you currently understand it. Set off in the direction you think is most likely, but commit to both learning more about yourself and having the courage to adjust your course if your purpose and work's requirements diverge. With awareness and courage, you will be able to find your purpose and fit your job to it. Ultimately, becoming indispensable does not require that your personal purpose and organizational mission align perfectly today, but instead that you are consciously on the path toward convergence and can make the emerging connections.

—————————— **Indispensable Solutions** ——————————

- Take time to reflect on your purpose. Pick up your journal, find a friend to talk to, or just go on a long, reflective walk. Consider these questions for hints: What did you love to do when you were younger? What would you do without being paid? If you could write a bestselling book, what would the message be?

- Another way to help identify your purpose is to write your obituary. Or, to be less morbid, write the introduction that a friend would give before you take the stage for a commencement address in twenty, forty, or sixty years. What are you going to talk about? Why are you a reputable speaker on that topic? What kind of a person are you? How would that friend describe how you have spent your life?

- It is shortsighted to think that your personal purpose should align exactly with your employer's mission statement ("I want to save orangutans, and they run a non-profit that funds orangutan sanctuaries in Borneo. Perfect!"). Instead, there are all sorts of ways that your personal purpose intersects with your work life—often in subtler and more meaningful ways. For example, if your purpose in life is to bring order to chaos, you could be anything from an operations consultant to a disaster relief worker. Alternatively, if your purpose in life is to protect the environment, you could be anything from an environmental lawyer to a green packaging engineer.

- Do not worry too much about having a consistent purpose across your work life and your home life. At times, particularly if you have children at home, these purposes may feel quite distinct (and sometimes even at odds). Start by finding what you can uniquely contribute to the world at large. Careers are long; indispensable employees know they can harmonize this professional purpose with other aspects of themselves over time instead of expecting perfect alignment in every moment.

2) Endorse the Campaign

In a modern democracy, electoral decisions can be bewildering. There is a bevy of issues to consider and a slate of candidates whose positions are not always easy to assess. As a good citizen, you understand the issues, read the candidates' platforms, and make a thoughtful decision. Though the reasoning behind your decision may have been quite subtle, your vote is not. By pulling the lever, punching the ticket, or filling the bubble, you are putting your entire vote behind the candidate of your choice.

Indispensable employees adopt this same level of wholehearted support for their employers' missions. They care about not only their particular job but also their organization, their mission, and everything else their work stands for. Having decided to take the job, they endorse the whole campaign.

It can be easy to align oneself with a well-articulated mission, particularly when it has a social bent (as in a nonprofit). The Greenpeace employee cares about saving the humpback whales. The Sierra Club employee owns a compass and hiking boots. And the PETA office worker eats vegan every day. But the need to endorse the organization's mission is equally relevant in the corporate world. Just like social crusaders fight for their causes, Starbucks employees should care about "inspiring and nurturing the human spirit" (likely while also enjoying a good cappuccino).

Beyond supporting the explicit mission, the best employees also align themselves with the values of their organization. While from the outside, the corporate world may seem like a bleak landscape of companies focused on profit alone, organizations embody a broad spectrum of cultural values. Based on its history, leadership, culture, and business necessities, each organization has a unique set of values and associated behaviors that make it unique. One company may prioritize trust, family, and compassion while another may prioritize excellence, innovation, and openness. Like the overarching mission, indispensable employees also find alignment with and then strive to embody the unique set of values at play in their organizations.

Take it upon yourself to know what your organization stands for, whether it is explicitly articulated in the mission statement or implicitly included in your culture. Support it to the best of your ability and fully endorse your organization's campaign.

Indispensable Solutions

- Take it upon yourself to really understand the culture of your organization. Read the mission statement. Review the core values. Look at the operating principles. And, more than anything, observe the behaviors of your peers and your leaders. Beyond the explicit mission statement, what values are consistently articulated and lived? Are these consistent with your personal values? Is this a place that you can fully endorse?

- Even if you cannot find a company whose mission and values perfectly fit your own, you can always find one that does not violate them. Understand yourself and seek the best fit possible.

- Go to company events. It is important to invest yourself not only in the mission of the organization but also in the culture and the spirit thereof.

- If it helps, put your commitment to the mission down in writing somewhere. Just write down why you like your job, why you care, and why you think it is important. Writing can bring clarity and commitment—or elucidate the fact that you are misaligned.

• When you become a member of your organization, wear your status with pride. Endorse what you stand for. Become an emissary for your organization, whether out recruiting new hires, attending an industry conference, or chitchatting at the PTA meeting.

3) Like Your Job

You cannot expect the high-level mission of your organization to get you through the day. In addition, you must like many of your day-to-day tasks. Whether you are starting up a virtual reality company, upgrading technology use in schools, or running internal training programs, you should enjoy the job itself. You need not like every moment of every day; to begin, if you enjoy your activities more than half of the time, you are doing better than most.

On the other hand, without liking your job, all the best work strategies in the world will come to nothing. You will not strive to achieve at a job that you would rather not do. You will not be incented to move up to do the next job in your organization. Your indifference—or even, your dislike—will shine through, indicating to your manager that, at the end of the day, you really could not be persuaded to care. It is hard to take pride in work you do not particularly like.

As someone with the potential to be indispensable, do not waste it on a job you do not care about. Like what you do, or find another job.

—————————— **Indispensable Solutions** ——————————

- Ask yourself some basic diagnostic questions to assess how much you like what you are doing: *Do I look forward to going to work most days? Do I enjoy what I do? Am I relieved to leave at the end of the day?*

- When assessing whether you like your job, be sure to take a sufficiently broad perspective on the question. Perhaps you just missed a promotion. Maybe you got into a spat with your manager over the quarterly report. Or perhaps you got stuck restocking the communal supply closet for the whole team. Do not let the most recent happenings affect your overall perspective.

- Every job has tasks that are sources of energy and tasks that are uses of energy. Imagine you have a personal energy meter. What gives you energy? What takes it away? Consider how you can maximize the tasks that give you energy and minimize the ones that drain it.

- Do not feel bad if you do not like your job. Though you were hired because the job seemed like a good fit for your skills, you have no obligation to enjoy it. If you have realized that a job is not for you, do not get down on yourself; just get moving. Onward and upward.

4) Stick to Your Moral Compass

While fully investing yourself in the mission of your organization, you are cautious of blindly following your manager's dictates. Indispensable employees realize that mindlessly executing their manager's requests is a dangerous habit to adopt. Though unlikely, your manager's orders could be mistaken, misdirected, or downright illegal. As an indispensable employee, you understand that while endorsing your organization's mission is important, letting yourself be directed without reflection makes you less valuable as an employee.

Instead of blindly following, indispensable employees ask themselves whether each action is right for themselves and right for their organization. Indispensable employees take it upon themselves to carefully consider their actions. They know that they as individuals are held responsible and that following orders has never been an acceptable excuse in front of any moral jury. The culprits in the Enron scandal, the WorldCom demise, and the Tyco brouhaha did not receive absolution because they were merely following orders. You are accountable for all your actions. Adhering to your own moral sensibilities is necessary to keep you satisfied with your job and performing at your peak.

Indispensable Solutions

- Do not confuse indispensability with immorality. One approach to making yourself *technically* indispensable might be to commit some dubious legal acts. You are better than that. Be wise to the *spirit* of indispensability (i.e., being so excellent that your employer needs and loves you) instead of the *rule* of indispensability (i.e., being literally unfireable either by hook or by crook).

- Take responsibility for knowing the rules. When you get pulled over by a cop, you cannot claim that you did not see the speed limit sign, had no clue you were in a turn lane, or never knew that you were supposed to stop at red lights. Ignorance is no excuse. Take the time to read the employee manual, the employment contract, and all the papers that HR made you autograph.

- Being moral can mean more than just following your own internal moral sensibilities. Many times, it means knowing the specialized rules of your industry, whether those are food safety standards, stock brokering regulations, or waste management guidelines. In other words, being rule-abiding in your job may not always be an entirely intuitive task wherein you consult your gut to figure out what is right; instead, it may require a knowledge of and adherence to external rules and regulations. Read up and get yourself familiar with your industry-specific code of ethics to make responsible decisions in your role.

- Though your seasoned colleagues may know the landscape of your organization far better than you, no one knows your moral code better than you. At the end of the day (and the beginning of the day and the middle of the day), you are the only one who is accountable for your words, actions, and decisions. Regardless of their experience, do not follow the lead of others unless the path looks right to you.

- Even if they are never put in writing, make sure you follow the foundational rules of any workplace: Do not steal from your employer. Do not disclose company secrets. Do not break any of the rules and regulations of your company and industry. End of story.

- Here is your litmus test: Imagine that your actions become the subject of a viral news report read by everyone from your grandmother to your manager. If you are not happy to have them publicized, you should reconsider your course of action.

- If refusing to follow orders due to your own moral objections becomes a career-limiting decision, you must be willing to face up to the consequences. In this case, leaving your job is often the best choice. It is difficult to be indispensable at an organization that you do not fundamentally respect. Plus, if there are serious ethical issues at stake, your former employer will likely fold up shop soon enough.

CHAPTER FOUR

Become Actively Curious

At the beginning of a new job, you may feel fairly helpless. You have never used these software programs before. You do not know the expectations for meetings or the standards for presentations. You even have problems finding the cafeteria.

You may have a long way to go toward building expertise, but you can accelerate the learning process now. Indispensable employees know that knowledge is power and the faster they can accumulate knowledge, the better off they will be. They actively listen, sponging up whatever information is floating around their environment. Beyond this, they actively seek out information, asking questions and reading up about their industry and company. Indispensable employees take it upon themselves to learn what they need to know to be successful in their job.

So, turn on your childlike curiosity—that part of yourself that wants to understand how everything works and incessantly asks "Why?" Then pair that youthful sense of discovery with your adult ability to integrate information into a sophisticated understanding of the world. Together, this approach will turn you into an informed, useful employee, catapulting you ahead of your more passive peers.

1) Start by Listening

Listening may seem easy. We listen to our parents on the phone. We listen to our favorite music. We listen to professors lecture. Yet however frequently we exercise the skill, we do not always listen with full presence and attention. Instead, we commonly find ourselves multitasking. We do the dishes while talking to our parents. We work while listening to music. We imagine what we will be doing over the weekend while the professor delivers her lecture.

As an indispensable employee, you need to cultivate your ability to listen with focus and intent. Unlike in your collegiate lectures, the notes from the discussions you have at work will not be posted online afterwards and you do not have a textbook to serve as a dependable reference. There are few fallbacks to provide you with information when your basic listening skills fail you. So, turn on and tune in to what your colleagues, customers, and compadres are saying. It matters and it deserves your attention.

––––––––––––––– **Indispensable Solutions** –––––––––––––––

* Turn off the voices in your brain. We often listen more to our own thinking than to what the counterparty in a conversation is saying. We spend our mental energy considering whether we agree or disagree, formulating our next comment, or wondering when the meeting will end. To improve listening, quiet this mental chitchat.

- Be open. Listen to what is said rather than what you want to hear. Be receptive to what other people want to communicate to you.

- Do not listen with just your ears; turn on all your senses to fully engage in what is going on. Pay attention to speed, tone, and body language to listen beyond the words.

- Listen for both what is said and what is left unsaid. What do the silences tell you? What do the omissions tell you?

- Repeat what you hear to confirm your understanding. "You said that the water levels are dangerously low and we need a new plan." "You are concerned about our ability to hire enough morticians in the third quarter." "I am hearing that the biggest threat to success is the Delhi weather."

- Ask specific questions to make connections and expand your understanding. "Does that mean that we should close the facility?" "What are the implications of the new product design?" "Who will be responsible for quality controlling the café car offerings?"

2) Ask the Dumb Questions Now

Though you are spending your time getting smart, there is still an expectation that you are the new guy and that, accordingly, you know very little. You cannot unjam the copier without covering your hands in toner, much less navigate the complex political situation in your company. You are a true novice.

As a novice, you have many disadvantages over your more experienced colleagues. But you also have this one distinct advantage: there is no expectation that you know what is going on. While expectations are low, take advantage of this narrow window of newness to ask all your questions—smart, dumb, and otherwise. Ask how things work here, even if you understand well how similar systems work elsewhere. When others are speaking, note acronyms, concepts, and information that you are unfamiliar with; make a point to follow up and clarify. Request advice from others, either regarding specific situations or just general wisdom. Even if you were hired for your expertise, you can still ask questions with impunity. It is far better to ask now than to pretend you understand.

--------- **Indispensable Solutions** ---------

- Regardless of who you are talking to, the glow of new-guy ignorance will cling to you. Everyone from the executive assistants to the accounting staff—everyone except perhaps other new guys—will know that you are a fresh face. Do not get offended when other people assume you do not understand. Do not be ashamed by your lack of tenure or try to minimize it. Right now, use it.

- Do not limit your scope. Be actively curious about everything. Ask any questions that, within the bounds of professional propriety, are appropriate.

- Understand the lay of the land now. As the newbie, everyone knows you are both unschooled in the ways of the organization and not yet embroiled in any of the dreaded office politics. Take this chance to understand the political landscape of your organization as well and then only become involved thoughtfully and purposefully (if at all).

- Ask not only what but why. Get to the next level of understanding while people are patient to explain it to you.

- It is often the simplest questions that are the most revealing. Abandon complex multipart questions designed to showcase how clever you are. Instead, pose simple questions that require complex answers. "What is hard about that?" "What is important about that?" and the perennial favorite "Why?" are all useful go-tos.

- Since you are asking all the dumb questions now, make sure that you take pains to listen to the answers.

3) Get Yourself Smart

Your first week on the job may seem slow. Maybe your manager has not had time to sit down with you and explain everything (or anything). Maybe you feel like you do not have enough direction. Or maybe you are just adjusting to your new lifestyle. Instead of sitting around feeling vaguely incompetent, spend this valuable time getting smart.

Start by getting smart on your industry. As a relative newbie, you will be surrounded by pros who may have spent dozens of years in maternity retail, health-care operations, or whatever field you have decided to enter. And though you may lack the experience to match them today, you can nonetheless start to build your knowledge base. Take the initiative to become as much of an expert on the industry as you can. Find the relevant news sources in your field, sign up for the newsletters, and read the industry publications.

Simultaneously, get smart on your company. Attack the annual report and the marketing information with a highlighter in hand. If your company is public, listen to the quarterly earnings calls, particularly tuning in to the questions the analysts ask. Bone up on your competitors' annual reports, using their performance to better understand your own organization. Click through each page of the website, mining it for insights on what your company does, what your management team cares about, and how your company presents itself to others.

Employees who take it upon themselves to actively seek out information are rare. As a result of taking the initiative, you may get credit for being quite smart, even though this may be the result of just being particularly diligent. Another benefit of taking the initiative to get smart is that you acquire a relatively unique and valuable perspective for a newbie. Most new employees focus exclusively on becoming good at their jobs; they narrow their focus to the task at hand. You, on the other hand, start simultaneously with the task at hand and the big-picture view. Due to your knowledge of your company and industry, you can already think like the indispensable employee you are striving to be, placing your work in a broader context than your peers.

In sum, as you start a new endeavor, you have the choice of passively absorbing information or proactively pursuing it. Be the employee who develops his curiosity and accelerates his understanding.

Key Questions to Investigate

Test your understanding. Can you answer these questions about your organization? If not, how might you find the answers? (Note that you can easily adapt any of these questions to organizations that are not profit-oriented. Simply consider your products and customers in a nonfinancial sense.)

- When was the organization founded and for what purpose?

- What was the founder's story and motivation?

- What are the major lines of business in the organization?

- Where do most of the organization's revenues come from?

- Where do most of the organization's profits come from?

- What market share does the organization hold in each of its lines of business?

- How profitable is each line of business?

- How profitable is each product?

- How does the business vary by geography?

- Who is the target customer?

- What is most important to the customers?

- What is the organization's competitive advantage?

- Why do customers choose this company over others?

- What are the essential functions the organization must get right to deliver on the value proposition?

- What is the biggest threat facing the organization?

- What are the two or three issues that keep management up at night?

- How are decisions made in the company?

- Who has the power in the organization?

—————— **Indispensable Solutions** ——————

- Replace your reading material. As you ramp up on a new job or project, replace some portion of your normal reading material (your online blog addiction, your Jane Austen novels, or your bathroom newspapers) with reading relevant to work.

- Take a peek at what your superiors and respected peers are reading. Are they flipping through *The Economist* or *Poultry World* in the office? Do they read *Us Weekly* or *Barron's*? A few minutes on Google or a consultation with a couple of colleagues will probably reveal the sources most useful for your line of work.

- Follow your high school English teacher's advice and actively read your materials. If you read hard copies, underline important points, highlight key takeaways, and write notes in the margins. Thoughtfully engaging in your reading will help you internalize the message more quickly.

- Effectively explaining an idea is great proof that you have internalized the concept. Be able to explain the fundamentals of your industry and company in terms that your neighbor or grandfather could understand.

- Instead of tiring yourself out constantly running down information, get the relevant facts pushed to you. Sign up for industry associations and trade groups that send out regular updates via email rather than trying to remember to visit their websites on a periodic basis.

- Find ways to continue to learn over time. Should you continue to read news and publications? Do you need to attend seminars or conferences? What will help you be in the know on an ongoing basis?

4) Study Your Situation

If you are like most people, you started your position with little more than a job description and are doing your best to impress based on that minimal guidance. Unfortunately, knowing that you need to "coordinate departments," "draft memos," or "analyze trends" is not enough direction. In fact, it is a bit like trying to find your way from Sunset Boulevard to Rodeo Drive with only a map of the solar system. You know that Rodeo is left of Mars, but after that, you are lost.

As you start out, try to study your situation as much as you can. Ask yourself: *What does it take to be an indispensable employee in my organization? And what does it take to be an indispensable employee in my particular role? How are individuals evaluated? What are the performance metrics?*

Similar to learning about your industry and company, you need to seek out information about your job; this includes not only the generalities that would help anyone in your organization succeed but the specifics about what your organization expects of someone in your position. Do your homework to understand as much as you can about the parameters for success as they apply to you.

—————— Indispensable Solutions ——————

- Ask people who have navigated the system for advice. Especially at the beginning, you can request guidance blamelessly. Find the model employees and ask them questions like "What advice would you give to someone just starting out?" "What is the one thing I should make sure that I do?" and "What has made you successful in the organization?" By asking veterans, you will find out not only how the system is intended to work but also how it actually does work.

- It can be tricky to ask for information on performance expectations before you have even put in a full month on the job. Start with the employee handbook and intranet to help you understand the broadly articulated expectations, then get more specific in conversations with your supervisor.

EXCEL AT EXECUTION

During the hiring process, your potential employer was primarily interested in your previous work and performance. While interviewing, you laid your past accomplishments on the table and hoped for the best.

Once you are hired and start working, it all changes. The achievements you depended upon during the hiring process turn into mere indicators of your likelihood to succeed, rather than your primary qualifications. You must show that you are the employee they hired you to be. Suddenly, you find yourself trying to type ninety words per minute. While transcribing for the CEO. In a client meeting. That is conducted half in Portuguese and half in Mandarin. (Perhaps you slightly exaggerated your skills on your résumé.)

While you may have promised the moon in your interview, the first tasks given to new employees are often uninteresting chores with a significant amount of supervision. You are asked to set up the room for the team meeting, make a playlist for the company off-site, or find a clip art banana for the department newsletter. Slam-dunking these first assignments, however inane, is the basis of being entrusted to do anything more sophisticated. Indispensable employees know this and apply themselves unhesitatingly. They build their reputations on consistently excelling at execution, regardless of the task.

Chapters 5–9 discuss how to become a highly functional employee, beginning with your first few assignments. You will learn to take direction thoughtfully, execute brilliantly, and communicate effectively. While these skills might seem to be simple, indispensable employees excel at these building blocks of their jobs.

CHAPTER FIVE

Set Yourself in the Right Direction

Your boss could be good or your boss could be bad. She could be the gifted manager who provides you with just the right balance of direction and independence. Or she could tell you to "figure out the second-quarter numbers" and leave you to muddle through them for far too long.

Employees who do the wrong thing are often not unintelligent or incompetent but instead misunderstand what they are asked to do, how they are asked to do it, or the relative importance of their different responsibilities. Indispensable employees, on the other hand, do not depend on their supervisor for effective direction; they take responsibility for what they are asked to do from the start, and do not allow their supervisor's instructions—or lack thereof—hinder their ability to become indispensable. They work to understand what their manager is asking for in both content and format. Once clear on the goal, they figure out their own approach. While working through their responsibilities, they take pains to prioritize appropriately and manage expectations on timing and delivery. They are wise to proactively check in early on in the project and course-correct as necessary. Ultimately, they deploy a suite of tactics to set themselves in the right direction, increasing their likelihood of success in all situations.

1) Understand What You Are Asked to Do

The first step to setting yourself in the right direction is knowing exactly what that direction is. While you may both think the instructions are clear, do not risk misunderstanding. Instead of saying yes and running off to do what you think you need to do, spend the extra two minutes to confirm your direction. It is your job, not your manager's, to take the responsibility for clarifying and confirming.

Clarifying your understanding of a request need not be time-consuming. Start by asking questions. Questions like "Are you talking about the Stevens case or the Kelly case?" and "Are you referring to that same brief we worked on last week?" can confirm that you are talking about the same subject. Then replay what you have been told by putting it in your own words to show that you understand. Reiterate using phrases such as "So, just to be clear, you want me to talk to Lane about ordering wallpaper for the new design project and then research emerging trends in coffee tables?" Make sure you know what you need to do, when you need to do it, and what the result needs to be before setting to work.

You will look far sillier when you return with a bottle of Hidden Valley Ranch when you were really asked for an appraisal of the property value of the Hide Den Valley Ranch, so clarify now.

————————— **Indispensable Solutions** —————————

- Though you do not want to exhaust your manager asking for excruciating how-to instructions, there is a level of detail that you do need. If you are told to analyze the budget, you do not yet have enough information to do so effectively. Over what period of time should you analyze it? Are you looking at your department, all departments, or the company as a whole? For what region of the world? Understand the level of detail necessary: time periods, organizational subdivisions, regions of the world, etc.

- Know the format of your output. Are you producing a bullet-pointed email, a forty-page thesis, or a PowerPoint presentation? Your level of effort and your approach will be markedly different based on what your output needs to look like. Confirm format with your manager up front—or, alternatively, confirm that format doesn't matter.

- Remember your fundamentals when taking directions (from way back in chapter 1, strategy 3, "Bring the Right Tools for the Job"): when receiving instructions, write it down, write it down, write it down.

- Try to understand your manager's ingoing hypothesis about the results of your work. "So, you expect to find issues in the Robinson account?" "You think that this quarter's net margin should be in the teens?" Understanding both the assignment and any expectations your manager has about the outcome will help you confirm that you understand not only the objective of your work but also the likely results. With this in mind, you will also be better equipped to spot problems in advance. (See also chapter 8, strategy 1, "Anticipate Roadblocks.")

2) Figure Out Your Own Approach

Determining what you need to do and in what order is often the hardest part of getting your work done. Should you draw up the seating charts, call the caterers, or confirm the flower order? Do you check the library, go on the internet, or call up an expert?

Remember that your manager is not your only resource in determining how to approach a specific task. In fact, your manager probably does not want to painstakingly spell out what you need to do on each assignment. Indeed, if he knew exactly how he wanted your job done and had the nitty-gritty details figured out, he would have told you. Or given you a painfully detailed manual. Or hired a programmable droid instead of a smart person like you. In most cases, he will not do that; instead, he wants you to use your creativity to figure it out yourself. It is up to you to balance limited direction from above with your own problem-solving abilities. This does not always mean that you have to invent the solution yourself, but rather that you have to draw masterfully on your resources to figure out how to approach the work at hand.

When starting a new assignment, quickly and creatively assess the resources at your disposal and assemble your game plan. How can you get your work done as efficiently and intelligently as possible? What resources can you draw upon: Company documents? Experts? Online resources? Whom should you consult for guidance: Your mentor? Your peers? Your crazy aunt Sue? Instead of running back to your manager for A-B-C instructions, identify your resources, do a bit of legwork, and problem-solve your way to the approach. As a rule, you should feel independent enough to figure out how to approach your work, but empowered enough to call on the right resources to help you do so.

—————————— **Indispensable Solutions** ——————————

- Even if your path seems unmistakably clear, take a second to think about your work before you dive in. Is there a more efficient way? How long should it take? Even if the approach is not rocket science, a bit of consideration before starting usually proves useful.

- Figure out who in your organization you can ask for high-value but low-stress help. It could be a peer. It could be a seasoned administrative assistant. It could be the guy who wanders around the office watering the plants. For every task, there is someone in your organization who has a perspective on how to do it. To avoid always asking your manager, discover the other people who have relevant experience.

- Remember that no man—and no organization—is an island. While you may feel confined within the three dividers of your cubicle and the four walls of your suburban office park, remember that there are billions of other people out there. They are not all doing exactly what you are doing, but they certainly know something. Looking for non-farm payroll? Call the Bureau of Labor Statistics. Looking for thoughts on how to format RFPs? Reach out to your friend who works in purchasing in a different industry. While you must be circumspect about confidentiality (as necessary), remember that there are plenty of people out there who have tackled a task like the one you are facing today. Consider how you can reach beyond the limits of your company to accelerate your learning.

3) Agree on Prioritization

If you have been appropriately comprehensive in not letting things fall off the table, you probably have a crazy list of things to do. This lengthy to-do list includes all those little things your manager mentions over tuna sandwiches, near the coffee machine, and at that awkward moment in the men's room. Which of all these to-dos comes first? Should you finish the monthly newsletter or research the Spanish Armada? Should you finish what you were working on before you ran into your manager at Starbucks or dive into his crazy new request?

As each new assignment is added to the list, be sure that you understand the relative prioritization of each piece of work. Completing less pressing or less important tasks first will only frustrate your manager. He will wonder why you do not understand what work is vital to your organization's survival and what work is simply "nice to have"—even if he has never communicated these priorities to you. Start by simply asking "Do you want me to do <your crazy new request> first or continue with <my current project> and get to this later?" If you cannot get clarity immediately, bring your list to your next one-on-one or commit it to memory so you can quickly get feedback when you run into him in the hall.

─────────── **Indispensable Solutions** ───────────

• Be flexible. When Oprah landed her first television gig, she did not continue working on her radio voice. No, she pulled up and reprioritized her time. Understand that priorities can change, and adjust your focus accordingly.

• When asked to do something, avoid responding with "I have <Other Project X> and <Other Project Y> to do first." Unless you are working on projects for multiple people, allow your manager the freedom of determining what is most important. A response of "I have other things to do" sounds too much like a no. Instead, engage in a dialogue of prioritization.

- Start honing your sense of relative prioritization. While you should always confirm your priorities with your manager, you need to start developing your own sense of what is most essential. Propose your own prioritization and ask them to confirm or deny instead of waiting to be directed.

- Remember that you can only ever really do one thing at a time. Aggressive prioritization of your to-do list is necessary not only to deliver on your supervisor's expectations, but also to focus your energies for maximum productivity.

- Force yourself to constantly reassess your prioritization. Start the day with a list of priorities of what you need to get done. Reprioritize as you progress through the assignment in particular and the day in general.

- If priorities change, make sure that you reset timelines (see the next section: chapter 5, strategy 4, "Manage Expectations"). If your efforts have been entirely refocused, inform your supervisor of the impact on previous timelines as soon as possible. As you have collaboratively prioritized your work, he should be sympathetic to these changing timelines.

4) Manage Expectations

Without realizing it, you and your manager can have very different perceptions of how difficult any given task will be. Your manager thinks it is the easiest thing in the world to analyze your company's candle sales through independent retailers for last quarter. She thinks, *That information is in the central ordering system, so it should be easy to do by end of day.* Sure enough, at 4:00 p.m., she will be awaiting your report.

You know, however, that the task may not be so easy. In your company, independent retailers do not routinely provide their point-of-sale data. When they do, they all send over their information separately so you have to meld them all into one massive file. Further, candle product codes are sometimes confused with candleholder product codes, so you have to sort through the entries manually. Unlike your supervisor, you know that the request is three days of hard work, minimum.

Without managing expectations, you are likely to work hard for those three long days and nights. Even if the output is stellar and you worked diligently the entire time, your manager might be disappointed that you delivered so belatedly. *Of course it is good,* your manager thinks. *She had three full days to get it done!* Everyone is frustrated with both the results and the process. Whether you knew the expected timeline or not, you were still judged against it.

Align expectations with your manager early on, if not while receiving the initial direction, then soon thereafter. Be clear and honest about how difficult the work will be and your resulting timelines. When you do good work, you should get credit for it, rather than risk having it misunderstood. And if you are misunderstanding an assignment or overcomplicating an approach, you need to know that now as well.

―――――――― **Indispensable Solutions** ――――――――

- Informing your manager of timing expectations has the added benefit of allowing your manager to reconsider whether any given task is a worthwhile investment. While it may make sense to spend an hour on a task, it may not make sense to spend a full day. Giving fair estimates of how long work will take can help your manager confirm that each task is deserving of the proportionate investment of your time and energy. Expectations and prioritization work hand in hand.

- **Do not just set timelines; drive them.** When you agree on a delivery deadline, you should be the one setting meetings and sending updates. Show that you have the logistics under control. If your manager is the type of person who likes to plan, he will feel better having a few check-in meetings in his calendar rather than wondering, *Weren't we going to review Rajesh's work on Friday?*

- The classic formulation of the idea of managing expectations is "underpromise, overdeliver." In other words, you should promise what you are confident you can do but strive to exceed that expectation on one or multiple dimensions—time, quality, or scope. Beware, however: while it can be impressive to overdeliver, avoid taking this theory too far. Consistently overdelivering may start your manager wondering if you ever give honest estimates of how long assignments will take or are sandbagging on everything.

5) Course-Correct Early On

You are shoving off from Rotterdam on a cruise across the Atlantic. Set off in one direction and you will end up in New York. Set off at only a slightly different angle and you will end up in Miami. Needless to say, New York and Miami are a world apart (and we are not just talking about weather here).

In other words, a tiny shift at the outset has a lot of impact; it can even completely change the outcome. On the other hand, take a similarly small shift later down the line and you will only end up in Atlantic City. Correcting your course early has a great effect and takes little effort; correcting your course later requires a much greater effort to achieve the same impact.

Instead of working diligently in the wrong direction, course-correct early on. After a brief period of working, check back in with your supervisor to make sure that you are headed in the right direction. This check-in need not be a full status update, but instead a quick heads-up on your expected course. Logistically, you can send an email with preliminary thoughts shortly into your allotted project time or catch your manager for a five-minute conversation between other meetings. No one wants to work for three weeks to find he has been focusing on the wrong issues. So, as you would navigating at sea, remember to check your course early on to avoid ending up at the wrong port of call.

Indispensable Solutions

- Only course-correct once you have made partial but meaningful progress. For example, say you are writing a white paper with your manager. If you share your approach for the paper and it matches what your manager dictated last Thursday word for word, you are not ready to course-correct. Your manager will think, *What did you spend the last day doing? This is exactly what I told you!* If you have taken the outline to the next level of detail, on the other hand, now is an appropriate time to check in before moving forward.

- Beware of asking your manager to double her workload by looking at a preliminary version of your full output. An appropriate course-correction should involve reviewing a briefer, simpler, or more pointed summary of your work—not reviewing a poor, undeveloped version of your final product.

- Useful phraseology for check-ins includes "I just wanted to follow up on <project> and confirm that I am headed in the right direction. I am planning on <summary of approach>." Then reiterate your timeline and priorities. Closing with a line like "I just wanted to confirm this is on track. Let me know if you disagree; otherwise, I will be working on the above." In case you do not hear back in a timely manner, you should default to moving forward instead of making your course-correction a barrier to progress.

- These moments of course-correcting are great opportunities to get early reactions that you can incorporate into your work. If feasible, ask your manager for not only confirmation of direction but any quick reactions she may have. Though you may be tempted to hold back your product until you think it is perfect, this is a high-risk/dubious reward strategy.

- If your manager pushes back on your desire to course-correct, back off. Since this is about getting your manager the product she wants, do not force her to check back in with you. She may be unwilling to review anything before you have put in the time.

CHAPTER SIX

Work Intelligently and Independently

When it comes down to it, work is work. However you present yourself, prepare, and invest yourself in the mission, at some point, you simply have to get stuff done.

When you buckle down to do the core tasks of your job, how do you do it? Do you close your eyes and blindly set to the task at hand or keep your brain engaged? Do you run in your own direction or confirm that you are on track? Do you end up with a preposterous answer or double-check to make sure your work is error free?

Indispensable employees work intelligently and independently to complete their work. They know that every task does not deserve the same effort and wisely scale their investment to the task at hand. Then, as they work, they ensure that they are working as productively as possible, continually refocusing their efforts on the most important issues. Finally, when finishing their work, indispensable employees make sure that their product is both error free and reasonable. They stay engaged throughout the process of working, refusing to turn off their brains as they simply execute by rote.

The following strategies will help you work intelligently and independently toward whatever assignment you have been given.

1) Scale Investment in Tasks

The Declaration of Independence begins with the line "We hold these truths to be self-evident, that all men are created equal . . ." While self-evident equality may be true of people, it is not true of work. In the work world, not all tasks are created equal. Some work is more important. Some work is less important. Some work needs a high level of precision and attention to detail. Some work requires only a broad, directional answer.

The indispensable employee adjusts her investment to the nature and relative importance of the assignment. She knows that time is not infinite and that it must be spent wisely. By scaling her investment, she can do more of the right work and avoid wasted effort.

Like many aspects of being indispensable, developing the judgment to do this well takes time and practice. Happily, it is not important that you know exactly how much effort to expend on any given task on day one. What is important is that you adopt a critical mindset from the start. Instead of blindly giving everything 110 percent effort, think closely about the task and scale your investment accordingly.

------------ **Indispensable Solutions** ------------

- One way to scale your investment to the importance of the task is to articulate your approach in terms of the time it would take. Many tasks might have a two-minute approach, a two-hour approach, a two-day approach, and a two-week approach. Make sure you are aligned with your supervisor on what level of depth is appropriate.

- For the less important tasks, ask yourself: *What is the minimum amount of work necessary to finish the job? Do I need to know the prices of all the varieties of eggs or only a representative sample?* Getting thoughtful representative samples can help you get to a quick answer that is both expedient and sufficient.

- Importance, urgency, rigor, and size of investment are four separate dimensions that help determine how and when you will tackle a task. Remember that urgent tasks are not always the most important. Similarly, the most important tasks do not always need a high level of rigor. Consider those dimensions to figure out how much time and energy to invest in each task.

- Resist the temptation to make things harder than they need to be. Sometimes a task is simpler than it initially seems. If the results are sufficient, do not reject the easy approach just because it is easy. For example, indispensable employees know that there are some questions that can be answered easily by asking one or two experts who will have *the right answer* instead of many people who have *an answer*; they embrace these more expedient methods.

2) Pump Up Productivity

Do not mistake activity for productivity. You could spend your whole day crunched over your computer, painstakingly tagging database fields as product or service sales, only to discover they will be analyzed together. There is a difference between being busy doing stuff and being busy doing the *right* stuff.

While working, watch for the telltale signs that you are being active instead of productive. You may find yourself answering every email in your inbox, including the particularly old ones. You may be drawn to finishing the least important items on your to-do list as you avoid the big task. Or you may find yourself busily executing without stopping to think. Often, shifting out of activity mode is simply a matter of realizing that you are in it.

Once you stop being merely active, you can focus on maximizing productivity. Find a system that works for you to organize your life. Set to the task immediately, and find the most efficient path for tackling it. Indispensable employees seek out the hacks that make them exceptionally productive in all aspects of life.

Indispensable Solutions

- Take time to develop expertise in the most common systems and applications you will use in your role. Make sure you take advantage of their built-in time-saving devices, such as shortcut keys, preprogrammed functions, and specialized tools. This may take a weekend investment in reading a manual, taking a tutorial, or simply spending hours watching YouTube videos, but it will speed you up over the long run.

- Make space to work without interruptions. Though you should remain accessible for important asks, you may need to carve out time and space away from your colleagues to maximize your own productivity. This may mean turning off your email, unplugging your phone, closing your office door, or temporarily relocating to a conference room to find a productive space. If nothing else, simply turning off notifications when you receive emails can go a long way.

- Be conscious of your procrastinatory urges. Becoming aware of how you are using your time and whether you are on the critical path is often half the battle. If you sense you are procrastinating, ask yourself: *What am I avoiding? What is getting in my way? What am I afraid of?* Seeing the situation more clearly can help you push through and get back on track.

- Just start. You may not have the perfect approach yet, but often you need to get going instead of waiting for the most brilliant way to tackle a challenge. For example, start by creating a draft instead of attempting to produce the perfect final product on the first go-round. Lower the bar to get yourself to begin.

- Take it bite by bite. Do not be the python that swallows the antelope and spends his whole day with massive indigestion. Instead of becoming paralyzed by the difficulty of completing an entire assignment at once, break your large tasks into digestible pieces that you can tackle with diligence and focus (e.g., "Look up telephone number for the supplier" versus "Fix issues with chemical orders"). Write these smaller steps on your to-do list instead of—or in addition to—the big ones. Each component should be well defined and actionable.

- You do not run the dishwasher every time you have one dish or do your whites every time you find a dirty pair of socks. Instead, you wait until you have a critical mass and do it all at once. Whatever your routine task, whether at home or at work, consider if it makes sense to wait until enough of it accumulates and deal with it all at one time. Just be aware that batch processing may not make sense in situations with many interdependencies or when you have time-sensitive deliverables—you know, when you really need those pants clean now.

- New day, new list. When wrapping up the previous day or first thing as you start in the morning, get out a clean sheet of paper and write a to-do list with only what you plan to accomplish that day. Leave off things you secretly know you will not accomplish until tomorrow or the weekend; they only make you feel overwhelmed and guilty. To add a self-developmental angle, list not only what you want to do that day but also how you aspire to be while doing it.

- Resist becoming beholden to your calendar, accepting whatever meeting invites come your way. Instead, take back your time and align it to your goals instead of falling victim to a death by a thousand meetings. Say yes or no to meetings based on whether they are in support of your broader responsibilities rather than automatically showing up. Make sure you discuss this approach with your supervisor to ensure that your vision of what is important matches hers.

- Ultimately, you should develop your own personal productivity system. There is an abundance of productivity advice out there and whole swaths of the bookstore devoted to the topic. Go beyond the fundamentals here and find the system that works for you.

3) Pull Up and Think

It is sometime after lunch, and your burrito is sitting in your stomach like a brick. Sadly, it is not only depressing your digestion, it is also dragging down your cognitive processing. Indeed, the next time you look up to the clock, it is 4:32 p.m. and you have easily spent three hours trying to track down monthly sales numbers from the second quarter of last year.

Was that a good use of your time? If you pulled up and thought about it after the first fifteen minutes, you probably could have figured out that (1) last year's numbers are not that important to your task anyway, (2) you probably are not going to find them, and (3) you are swearing off Tex-Mex food until next month.

Indispensable employees make a point of frequently pulling up and thinking about what they are doing. They shake themselves from screen-induced comas to figure out whether they are still doing the right thing, in the right way, for the right reasons. They refuse to become a cubicle-contained zombie, thoughtless and disengaged.

Pull up, step away from the details, and check in that you are still doing the right work in the right way.

—————————— **Indispensable Solutions** ——————————

- Take advantage of the natural breaks in your work flow. A quick break between sequential steps in your work can be a good opportunity to reassess whether you are still headed in the right direction. This can also be a suitable time to reprioritize (see chapter 5, strategy 4, "Agree on Prioritization").

- Set alarms. If you are having problems getting your head out of your work, set external alerts at periodic intervals (e.g., at every fifteen, thirty, or sixty minutes) to get yourself to check in. Alternatively, set alarms for whenever you think you should be done with a given piece of work. Choose your weapon: smartphone alarm, Outlook appointment with yourself, or egg timer.

- Though we all know the quote as "I think, therefore I am" (*"Cogito ergo sum"* for the high school Latin junkies among you), the full quote is "I doubt, therefore I think, therefore I am." And while we are not tackling fundamental metaphysical questions here, Descartes has a good point. When you pull up to think, you can also adopt a critical frame of mind. Engage your brain more fully by not only turning it on, but also by asking honest and even harsh questions about your approach and the interim results. Think to yourself: Is there a better way of doing this? Why do I believe this is leading to the right result? How could this be wrong? What other questions should I be asking? Be willing to get honest with yourself when you pull up and think.

- Ultimately, you are looking for the point of diminishing returns. When do you have enough of an answer to move forward? How would you change your path forward based on what you know now? When does your continued investment in the task stop making sense?

4) Stamp Out Errors

You are smart. You are increasingly competent. And you spent a long time doing whatever it is that you were supposed to do for your manager. Given your serious awesomeness and significant investment, do not shoot yourself in the foot with silly mistakes. Instead, ruthlessly and mercilessly stamp out errors.

The problem with flawed execution is that it undermines all your other good work. If your manager can spend three minutes perusing your output and find an error in your work, she will assume that spending thirty minutes reviewing it will only reveal proportionally more errors (even if she found the only error there). Unfortunately, if your manager starts to question your ability to execute the basics of your job well, you will not get points for all the effective communicating and good thinking you did on top of it. It is like golfing a twelve on the eighteenth hole; the benefits of all those earlier birdies immediately disappear.

Instead of falling victim to this trap, use your time as you did (or should have) on high school standardized tests: When you reached the end and had extra time, you went back to double-check your work. You made sure you understood the questions correctly. You made sure you entered your answers accurately. You knew that even if you had the right answer but marked it incorrectly, it would be counted wrong, wrong, wrong. So, you checked and rechecked.

—————————— **Indispensable Solutions** ——————————

- What differentiates the indispensable employee from the run-of-the-mill employee is the former's ability to not only check for errors but to do so quickly and efficiently. They know that double-checking does not mean doing all their work a second time. Instead, indispensable employees use shortcuts to check their work in the most time-efficient way possible. Read your work back out loud to help you spot textual errors. Check key numbers like totals, means, and medians. If the same number shows up multiple places, make sure all instances match. Spot the places where you can do quick math to confirm a more complex calculation. Look for patterns as well as potential deviations from the pattern.

- Listen to the Jackson Five: "A, B, C, it's easy as one, two, three." Hit the spell-check button.

- If you have time after spell-checking, read over your work once more to make sure you are not missing the mistakes that may betray how heavily you depend upon Microsoft programs to support your command of the English language. Read for homonyms that many people easily interchange: they're, there, and their; complement and compliment; effect and affect. You are smarter than a fifth grader, so show it.

- Many email systems have the ability to add an automatic delay on all outgoing messages. Once you set up the rule, all outgoing messages will stay in your outbox for the proscribed amount of time before they're sent, allowing you to reopen them, edit them, or fully delete them. Even just a minute's delay can keep you from accidentally sending a half-written reply or give you a moment to reconsider a hastily written note.

- Despite thoroughly checking their work, even indispensable employees make mistakes. The difference, though, is that indispensable employees take responsibility for their mistakes, raise their hands for help, and fix what needs to be fixed. They reflect upon the situation to learn both what could have gone differently this time and what broader lesson is at stake. They move forward swiftly, refusing to let these rare errors destroy their confidence. (For strategies on this, navigate to chapter 8, strategy 3, "Put Your Hand Up When You Need Help.")

5) Reality-Check Your Work

It has been a long day in the office, but you are finally done with an honest day's work. You have focused on the right tasks, figured out your own approach, thought broadly about answering the whole question, and kept your mind engaged throughout. You have been effective in not only getting stuff done but in getting it done well. As you close your laptop, you glance back at the financial statements you pulled together; you have projected that your company will earn twenty-seven trillion dollars next year. All your hard work aside, you immediately realize that revenues greater than GDP cannot possibly be right.

While checking your work for explicit mistakes, also make sure that your results pass the sniff test. Think about what you know about the world generally and about this question specifically to determine whether your conclusions are within the realm of reasonability. Reality-checking is important for both quantitative and qualitative conclusions. If your notes tell you that 80 percent of attendees to the PETA convention banquet have ordered the steak option, it may be worth double-checking your records. If your work tells you to target twelve- to seventeen-year-olds for your new line of denture cream, you may have missed something.

Equally important, you should reality-check the feasibility of implementing anything you recommend against the political landscape of your organization. If you are suggesting that your manager cut the advertising budget for your flagship product, you may run into issues with the marketing department. Similarly, suggesting scaling down your CEO's pet project may not go over too well. Without abandoning honesty and integrity, you can at least show that you are aware of the context and strive to offer solutions that are reasonable for your organization.

———————— **Indispensable Solutions** ————————

- Eliminating errors and reality-checking your work are two strategies that are subtly but importantly different. In error checking, you ask *Did I do it correctly?* while in reality-checking you ask *Does the answer look right?* The first focuses on process and requires technical expertise while the second focuses on output and requires judgment. Combine both to be fully effective.

- For quantitative conclusions, check to make sure your answer is the right order of magnitude (e.g., millions instead of trillions in sales). Alternatively, you can often do some quick math to confirm that your answer looks right. For example, if your company earned twenty-seven trillion next year, what percent of the market would it have? More than 100 percent market share? Something is wrong.

- Keep a couple of frequently used and commonsense figures in the back of your head to make reality-checking numbers easier. These could be anything from your department's budget to your company's profits, or from the industry's revenues to the country's GDP.

- Sometimes, the reality check you need to run is not on the appropriateness of the answer, but instead on the feasibility of implementation. Ask yourself: *Will people in the organization really go along with my proposal? What would be required for them to support it? Is that realistic?* Thinking through the angles will help you avoid proposing a solution that is obviously politically unwise.

CHAPTER SEVEN

Communicate Effectively

The value of flawlessly executed work and expansive thinking can be nullified if an employee's communication is confused. Indispensable employees know that communicating with their managers is not about just explaining what they did all week and justifying their paychecks. Nor is their communication something that happens haphazardly when their work is complete. Indispensable employees know that effective communication is part of the work itself.

As such, indispensable employees are intentional about their interactions. They bring context so their counterparties understand how their communication fits into the bigger picture. They bring purpose, ensuring they know why they are there and getting the answers they need. They often adopt a "bottom line up front" structure, sharing the most important information immediately. Finally, they adapt their communications to their audience and share their key insights in a way that will be heard.

1) Start with Context and Purpose

Your manager has a lot on his mind: He is thinking about the department's gap to budget. He is thinking about his lunch meeting with purchasing. Even though he does not particularly like basketball, he is thinking about why his alma mater never makes it past the Sweet Sixteen and ruins his March Madness bracket every year.

You walk into his office. You have done great work and nailed your assignment. But sadly, your manager may have no idea how your work fits into his much broader world. Does this affect his budget, his lunch meeting, or his March Madness bracket?

When communicating, start with context. Remind your manager (or, as applicable, all the meeting attendees) why you are there and what you are doing. Reground them in the trajectory of your work and how this meeting fits into the broader plan. Then bring purpose. Be clear in your own mind and with others about what you need to accomplish in this engagement. Is your purpose to inform of developments, discuss a hard-to-solve problem, brainstorm creative solutions together, or drive to a decision? Articulate the purpose and structure the meeting accordingly (see the next strategy, "Adopt the 'Bottom Line Up Front' Structure," for more). As you conclude, make sure you come back to your original purpose and ensure you have achieved your objectives. Finish again with the context of what will happen next.

──────────── **Indispensable Solutions** ────────────

- Be explicit with your purpose. Do not hesitate to start every form of communication with a line as direct as "The objective of this meeting/weekend retreat/secret cabal is to . . ."

- Be clear on not only the purpose of the conversation but also the roles that each of you will play in reaching your objectives. Who is the decision maker? Who has input to the decision? Who will execute it? Be clear in your own head and be explicit with others to speed the process and keep things on track.

- Know your needs. Whatever you require—revised time-lines, budget approval, input on a prototype—do not leave without it. Circle back as needed at the end of the conversation to make sure you have what you need.

- One of the greatest tools in your indispensable arsenal is an agenda. A thoughtful agenda helps translate your purpose for meeting into the minutes you spend together. Many people write agendas with vague topics and little sense of purpose, listing items like "Capital Planning" or "Hair Net Reorders." Instead, write your agenda as a verb-led set of bullet points: "Brainstorm Next-Generation Tater Tots" and "Decide on Final Ketchup Recipe." Using verbs helps you be clear on whether each topic is for information, consultation, or decision. Also consider adding estimated time allotments and roles of who leads each part of the meeting. Depending on how your organization feels about printing, you may want to bring hard copies and distribute to participants.

2) Adopt the "Bottom Line Up Front" Structure

Bottom line up front. BLUF. It is not a tactic for your online poker games, but instead a key skill in communicating clearly. Unlike keeping your answer hidden behind a stern poker face, bottom line up front requires you to lay all your cards on the table at the beginning. Your bottom line is included at the beginning of any interaction—in the first few lines of an email or the first few minutes of a meeting. This bottom line is not a recap of the entire situation or the process you used to get there, but instead the essential message germane to the topic at hand.

Though the BLUF structure is said to have originated in the military, it finds broad use today. Here is an example of using bottom line up front in a live update with your manager:

- First, lay out your approach for the meeting. You remember to bring context (see chapter 7, strategy 1, "Start with Context and Purpose") and begin by reminding your manager what else has happened and how this fits in. You also bring purpose, being clear about the goals for today and what you need by the end of the meeting. This should be a couple of quick sentences, such as "I wanted to meet today to talk you through the design and budget for the new pineapple plantation in Kauai. There are three parts for us to review: the fields, the warehouse, and the canning factory. I need your agreement on the details. If these make sense to you today, I'll take them to Mr. Dole for final approval next week."

- Second, deliver your bottom line. Your bottom line will likely address what your manager is thinking about most. Do not make him wait for the answer (otherwise, you are likely to be interrupted by the question or he may impatiently flip forward in your materials). Continuing with the last scenario, here's an example of what you might say: "Before we start reviewing the three design components, I know you are probably wondering about the total cost of the plantation project. We can go through the details in each section, but initial estimates come out to forty million dollars." This is a much preferable approach to keeping your manager hanging as you slowly unveil the cost of each of the three segments. Unless the topic is particularly sensitive, put your bottom line at the beginning.

- Third, delve into the details of your work to the extent that your manager is interested. Use the agenda you shared at the outset to help you walk through each topic in a structured way and to keep you on track. You can recount more detail on the pineapple fields, the warehouse, and canning factory respectively. Cover each topic sequentially, allocating time based on your colleagues' level of interest. If they are not interested in going deeper, cover your key points, bring up your essential questions, and move on.

- Finally, be clear about decisions, implications, and next steps. Do not leave the meeting without fulfilling the purpose that you so carefully laid out for the interaction. Bring the discussion back to get what you originally needed (e.g., "So, what concerns do you have about the plan?"). Once you get the input you need, be clear about what you will do next to keep the project going in the right direction: "Given your concerns about the plantation budget, I will review the numbers with the team and get a revised quote to you by our meeting next Wednesday." Finish by confirming how and when your manager would like to reengage.

In this way, you have not just spewed a bunch of information; you have structured a conversation to give your manager what he needs in a digestible format. Simultaneously, you have also received the direction you need to stay productive and push your work forward.

——————————— **Indispensable Solutions** ———————————

- Bottom line up front is particularly useful when communicating via email. Assume that the recipient may only read the first couple of sentences of your note, and put the most important information at the beginning of your email. That way, the essential point will show up in a preview screen and catch the recipient's eye as they skim through their stuffed inbox.

- Though you should approach all your meetings with a clear structure in mind, you should also be flexible enough to go with the flow. Pause and give your manager more detail if he is interested in the nitty-gritty. Be prepared to take off on tangents that your manager finds interesting and relevant. Though you are the helmsman who happens to be at the wheel, your manager remains the captain who can redirect the ship at any time.

- Consider when you might want to stray from the bottom line up front format and put the answer at the end. This is often the case when extensive background is needed to understand the answer or the answer may be controversial.

3) Be Concise

Your workday is filled with drama. No, this does not mean that you are at the center of office politics or ride the emotional roller coaster of your colleagues' social lives. Instead, it means that when describing your work, you often make it sound like you are recounting swashbuckling adventures on the high seas: "Well, first I went to Bob from accounting to get the accounts receivable database. But Bob said that he only had an old version of the materials. So instead of using that, I went to Omar, who runs the data warehouse, and asked him to pull a more recent version for me—one that included this month's accounts. He sent me the database two days later because he was backed up with requests, but the file turned out to be too big to download on my system. So, on my way to lunch, I took him a jump drive to download the data straight to—" Blah, blah, blah.

Fascinating. You have effectively recited your entire schedule to your manager. And you have told him absolutely nothing.

Do not assume that the pseudodrama of your workday requires high-adventure storytelling. In most communications, the nitty-gritty details of what you did are the least interesting part of your message. Your manager is almost certainly less interested in learning how you got the database on your computer than in knowing how big the accounts receivables balance is.

Be concise and to the point. Though you should be prepared to go deeper when asked, you should preliminarily screen out most of the annoying logistical and procedural details. Most often, unless they indicate a broader break in the system, they simply do not matter and thus do not need to be communicated in relation to the matter at hand.

Indispensable Solutions

- Beware of communicating chronologically. As per the example above, chronological accounts of actions tend to degenerate quickly into "what I did today" stories instead of effective communication. Save these for the dinner table with your spouse, not the conference table with your manager. Your communication should be consistent and logical but not necessarily chronological.

- Become friends with bullet points. Bulleted structures introduce easy organization into your communications. Not only does the short, fragmented structure of bullet points help you keep each thought to the point, but the indentation also helps you organize your information into levels of primary, secondary, and tertiary importance.

- Often, employees want to share the details of what they have done in order to get credit for their efforts. While managers can be struck by the unexpected difficulty of a task you have completed, they frankly expect you to figure things out as you go. As an effective employee, you should be an independent problem solver who can complete the work that has been asked of you, so a little troubleshooting here and there is nothing to brag about. Indeed, boasting about all your toils shows a dangerous preoccupation with activity over results. So, instead of communicating your process, focus on the impact.

- Consider how to be concise in different mediums. In voice-mails, for example, there is an even higher requirement for the caller to be concise given the one-sided delivery of information. Leave the most important information first. Ensure that you speak with crystal clarity. Do not hesitate to rerecord.

- When speaking, eliminate filler words like "um" and "ahh." Cleaning up your word choice helps you sound more confident in your message.

- Reread your written communications before sending them. What can be taken out without affecting the essence of the message? Remember that you are no longer in college;

there is no motivation to stretch your writing to meet a certain word count. In the working world, brevity is valued.

- While your communication is concise and to the point, you should still have all the related details in your back pocket. Be ready to provide depth and detail when requested, including backup calculations, sources of information, and detailed methodologies.

4) Adapt Your Approach to Your Audience

One boss, two boss, red boss, blue boss: Much like Dr. Seuss's fish, not all bosses are the same. In fact, they can be curiously different. One likes to review all your work beforehand and then hold brief meetings to deliver his well-considered feedback. Another responds to all your questions on the fly and never likes to have meetings on his calendar. And a third seems to say yes to everything you propose, refusing to review your work and making you nervous that you are not getting enough oversight. Before talking to your supervisor, think about the way that he likes to interact. Adapt your communication style by thinking through his preferences along a few key dimensions:

- *Preparation*: What does your manager like to see before the meeting? Does he like to review an agenda? Or does he like to go through the materials you will present in advance so he can be prepared to give you feedback?

- *Style*: Does your manager prefer unidirectional show-and-tell or to engage in dialogue? Does your manager want to have you lead the discussion, or would he prefer to question you? Does he prefer that you make a big presentation, or is that overly formal?

- *Common Understanding*: Does your manager know a lot on the subject that you are addressing? Do you need to bring him up to speed on the topic first? Can you use acronyms that he is familiar with, or should you explain them the first time around?

- *Depth of Support*: What does your manager need to see to believe your arguments? Does he just want the answer, or would he prefer to dig into the details of how you got there? Is it important to cite your sources? Do you need to explain your methodology and approach, or is he more interested in your conclusions?

- *Format*: How does your manager prefer to see your work? Should you bring the model of the boutique hotel you are designing? Would he prefer to see a PowerPoint presentation? Should you bring printouts of your Excel sheets? How will your manager best engage in your materials?

Communicating effectively is not about saying what you want to say, how you want to say it. Communicating effectively is about saying what your audience needs to know and in a way that they will hear it.

————————— **Indispensable Solutions** —————————

- You do not need to get out your Magic 8-Ball to divine the answers to the questions raised in this section. Instead, you can often just ask your supervisor about his communication preferences. He will likely appreciate that you are being accommodating, and you will increase your likelihood of a positive outcome by communicating in a format that your manager can easily digest.

- Communication preferences are often reflective of broader management style; someone who is hands-on, accessible, and caring may prefer texts and expressive emojis whereas someone who is more introverted, reflective, and deliberate may prefer emails that they can digest independently. In addition to asking, reflect upon your manager's broader management style for clues.

- Abandon your expectations; many managers have communication preferences that may surprise you. Some are properly formal and will look down upon your use of acronyms via text. Others might just teach you a thing or two about using emojis on Messenger. Default to a more formal style, but tailor your message as you discover what is most effective.

CHAPTER EIGHT

Tackle Problems Head-On

Odysseus, the protagonist of the Greek epic *The Odyssey*, spent ten years of his life trying to reach his hometown of Ithaca. The trip was not an easy one to say the least. Over the course of his journey, he braved a colony of cannibals, a witch who turned half his crew into pigs, and a one-eyed monster that tried to eat him. Not exactly a walk in the park.

Although you are unlikely to run up against such life-threatening roadblocks in your career, you will face your fair share of issues. You will be unable to find the information you need. You will miscalculate a budget number. You will forget to tell your manager the cost of a new part before putting in the order. And then you will want to scream at the vendor who failed to bring your delivery on time and delayed your entire project.

It is impossible to avoid issues entirely. You will make mistakes, and others will make mistakes for which you will be held responsible. Happily, avoiding issues is not your job. Instead, your job is to handle issues as responsibly as possible. Like

Odysseus, you need to keep your cool in the face of troubles, navigating around all obstacles to achieve your goal. Learn the strategies of this chapter to help you navigate between your versions of Scylla and Charybdis.

1) Anticipate Roadblocks

Anticipating roadblocks is the most valuable (though not always feasible) strategy for dealing with problems. Instead of waiting for an issue to crop up, you think critically about the path you need to take and anticipate problems along the way.

To do this, first work to identify issues in your own process. Ask: What could take more time than expected? What could be more difficult than expected? What else could possibly go wrong?

Next, think about the interdependencies you have with others. Ask: What do I need from other people to complete my work? Do I need input? Information? Agreement? Do I know who will provide these? And further, do they know that I am dependent on them? How likely is it that they will deliver what I need? What competing demands for time and resources may get in the way?

With this extensive list of potential roadblocks, you can wisely decide how to mitigate each. Should you build more time into the work plan, check in on a colleague's progress, or raise the issue to your superior? Identify the mitigating actions for each issue and make sure they are on your to-do list (or someone else's).

It is best to get in the habit of looking for roadblocks and checking back on mitigating actions periodically. Update meetings with supervisors often provide a good trigger for revisiting roadblocks. Mentioning potential roadblocks and the steps you are taking to avoid them should become a key piece of your update meetings.

--------- **Indispensable Solutions** ---------

- In most large organizations, very few major projects have not been attempted at least one time (and sometimes many times) previously. Ask company veterans who the previous project leaders were and seek out their advice. With any luck, you will avoid the biggest roadblocks they faced the last time around.

- Sometimes the roadblock does not come when you are doing the work but when you are socializing the ideas to gain support in your organization. Think through the interpersonal dynamics of the reception of your work. Ask: Who might disagree with my conclusions? Can I get these people to give input so they are more likely to agree with the outcome? What might be hard for them about accepting or endorsing my work? What are they afraid of?

- Running up against a roadblock is typically a losing situation. But sighting a pitfall in advance and avoiding the issue turns the potential loss into a relative win. Indeed, sometimes just spotting the iceberg in advance is enough to make you the hero. With sufficient lead time, you may expend very little effort to transform a potential pitfall into a nonissue.

2) Offer Solutions, Not Problems

There is a little ledger kept in the back of every manager's head. You can imagine it as a quaint little T-account that balances the solutions (the credits) and the problems (the debits) that you dump on her desk. Are you a problem solver? (Credit!) Or do you merely identify problems, get nervous about them, and pass them on to your manager to provide guidance? (Debit!)

Presenting problems makes you look lazy and helpless. Presenting solutions, on the other hand, makes you look proactive and positive. Instead of throwing your hands up at the sight of trouble, take responsibility for the problems you identify. Start by asking yourself: If I were my manager and had to solve this problem, what would I do? What options do I have? What are the plusses and minuses of each alternative? If I had to choose, what course of action would I pick?

When you begin proposing solutions yourself, you may soon realize that supervisor was not the answer-spouting oracle you thought him to be. Sure, he is more experienced than you, but some of the time he is just using logic to think about what the best solution should be. When proposing your own solutions, you can similarly start by being a logical thinker and then develop your judgment over time.

Indispensable Solutions

- Never propose just one answer. Instead, come up with a handful of ways of attacking the problem and lay out the relative benefits and drawbacks of each. Then highlight the one that you would suggest without becoming too attached to it. The goal is to offer multiple solutions and have a good conversation to pick the path forward, not just focus on one great idea.

- Once you determine a couple of angles on the problem, you should invest to communicate these clearly to your manager. Try an approach like the following (in fun, Mad Libs format): "The issue is that [*organizational issue*] our building is overrun by vampires. I think we should [*proposed solution*] <u>distribute garlic to employees</u> because [*rationale*] <u>it is the most cost-effective solution at $2.69 per employee</u>. A second option is [*less attractive solution*] <u>distributing wooden stakes</u>, but [*rationale*] <u>treatment for splinters is not covered under our health plan</u>. Thus, I suggest [*awesome solution*] <u>garlic</u> for the [*issue*] <u>vampire</u> problem. Your thoughts?" Now assuming your manager is not already a vampire, this format will probably be met with a positive response. Your manager will appreciate that not only did you identify the vampire problem, but you also solved it all by yourself.

- Indispensable employees know that hesitating to solve a problem and passing it on to another only undermines their status as a fully responsible employee. Do not abandon your work when the going gets tough. Your manager wants to see you as someone who can be in charge while all is going well and who also stays steady at the helm when problems arise.

- Ask yourself: *Are there any broader lessons to be learned from solving this problem? Does it point to a broader issue in the system?* When possible, translate what you learn from solving one specific issue into a broader takeaway. You may raise your own awareness to spot the same issue in the future, identify a bigger problem in the organization, or find a greater personal insight for yourself. Turn problems into learning opportunities. (Refer to chapter 11, strategy 2, "Evolve the System," for more on how to capitalize on problems.)

3) Put Your Hand Up When You Need Help

You just spent four hours in your biggest customer's office, getting yelled at about everything from irregular delivery times to botched batches of product. You left bleary-eyed, exhausted, and debating whether to just mail in your employee ID badge from the airport en route to Bali.

Maybe you made a mistake somewhere along the line to precipitate this all, or maybe you did not. Either way, there is a big issue now and you are terrified about how to deal with it. The possible plans of attack you have come up with include (a) curling up in a ball and hiding under your desk, (b) leaving for lunch and never coming back, and (c) pretending that you have suddenly contracted meningitis and request to be quarantined in your cubicle. In your gut, though, you know that you must face up to the issue. But how do you deal with it? What is plan D?

Instead of cowering in the corner or trying to cover up the evidence, raise your hand for help. Taking the initiative to raise your hand has multiple benefits: First, it helps relieve you of the unique burden of responsibility. You may want to deal with the issue all on your own, but situations like this are exactly why your manager is there. Second, since your manager is in the mix early, she can help avoid the situation getting out of hand—and do damage control if it does. Just imagine how much worse things could have gotten if this client decided to call your other accounts and share his choice thoughts about your service. You will want your manager to help you to pro-actively troubleshoot the issue instead of hearing about it from another customer.

Often, the biggest challenge in raising your hand for help is getting over the fear of what will happen when others find out about your mistake. In the moment, it can be hard to face that fear and hold your center; even if you are not at fault, the issue can feel deeply personal. It can be hard to maintain your confidence that, even though you screwed up, you are still a competent and worthy employee. Wise managers know to separate fixing the mistake from identifying who is at fault—and they know the mistake must be fixed first. Happily, after you put up your hand for help, they are there to help fix it, so you do not have to carry the load alone.

Be brave and address the issue. Put up your hand and ask for help before it is too late. Ensure your manager is never surprised.

Indispensable Solutions

- Everyone has their strengths. Everyone has their weaknesses. Sometimes you must raise your hand not because you run into a big issue but simply because you need help to complete your work. Recognize your weaknesses and be willing to ask for support when they impact your responsibilities. If you have worked enthusiastically toward completing your project and exploited your strengths to the best of your ability, you should not be faulted for honestly and humbly asking for help when you need it. When asking for help, though, be sure that you ask with sufficient time remaining so you can still complete your work on schedule.

- Think of that adorable little bear cub you found abandoned in the woods and wanted to raise in your woodshed. He may look charming and harmless now, but he will inevitably grow into the wild beast he was born to be. Covering up issues at work puts you in a similar situation to hiding a bear cub in suburbia. It may seem manageable now, but it can easily grow into a massive problem that you cannot keep under control. Give your bear to the zoo now, before he rips up your new leather couch, raids your fridge, and mauls your girlfriend. In other words, admit to the issues that you know could become big before they get out of control.

- There is no need to be dramatic when problems occur. Instead, take a deep breath and present the issue clearly, calmly, and logically.

- Take appropriate responsibility and avoid placing blame. If a problem comes up in your domain, your manager will be aware of the factors that are out of your control. Take responsibility for your piece and resist the temptation to point the finger at other people. Focus on solving it and moving forward.

4) Adapt Easily

From Thomas Edison's first recording of "Mary Had a Little Lamb" to the nascent years of rock and roll, records were the reigning format for audio consumption. Eclipsed only when 8-tracks hit the scene in 1966, their reign lasted over fifty years. Since then, things have changed more and more quickly. Compared to records' decades-spanning popularity, the 8-track lasted under twenty years, retiring soon after Sony put out its first Walkman in 1979. Cassette tapes had an even shorter life span, tossed by CDs in just ten years. And digital recordings came to rival CDs in less than a decade.

Not only in the world of audio technology but across the board, the world is changing. This is nothing new. The difference now is that the pace of change is accelerating. Circumstances change faster, more frequently, and more drastically than they ever have before. Your company's organization structure, ownership, processes, and customer expectations can shift just as quickly.

To be clear, change itself is not an issue. But employees' reactions to change can create big challenges. Whether your organization is facing a merger, your department has a new boss with a bothersome managerial style, or your customers are demanding new and unprecedented services, you need to adapt. As an indispensable employee, you adapt easily. You do not create issues by being the inflexible, inadaptable one. Instead, you are open to positive change and nimble to incorporate it. You adapt to change and help others do so as well.

Indispensable Solutions

- Expect change instead of constancy. If you can shift your expectations and come to see constancy as the surprise, integrating change will become easier.

- Change takes an enormous amount of energy. Unfortunately, you have only a finite amount of energy to dole out between all areas of your life—personal, professional, and otherwise. If things are changing in other spheres, you may well have less energy to expend on the change your organization demands. Think holistically about all the moving pieces and be realistic about what you can handle.

- Do not blindly accept change. While you are open-minded and flexible, it is also important that you thoughtfully consider the direction and impact of any change. Understand it fully. Think through the variety of impacts. Develop an opinion on how you think the change will impact the organization and its people.

- Often, the most difficult part of change is not letting go of the old or embracing the new but instead navigating through the uncertainty that sits between the two. While you may not fully know the new state of the world, hold on to what you do know: the timeline for future layoffs, the schedule for progress updates, or the process for sharing concerns. Take comfort in the small certainties while letting the unknown be unknown.

- If facing an uncertain situation, try some worst-case scenario planning. Often, even given the biggest changes at work—mergers, layoffs, and reorganizations—the worst-case scenario is that you may lose your job and be forced to find another. As an indispensable employee, you know that you will rebound quickly and confidently from such setbacks. Imagining the worst and accepting that as a real possibility can help calm your fears about how the future may turn out and help you find an interim peace with not knowing.

CHAPTER NINE

Take On Conflict Productively

At some point in your career, you will get mad. Fighting mad. Even Fighting Irish mad. And like the fierce Notre Dame mascot, you will want to straighten your leprechaun hat, put up your dukes, and start swinging.

Yes, in addition to dealing with problems that come up while working, you will also have to deal with interpersonal issues. You will face friction with your cubiclemate over the printer. You will have shockingly impassioned arguments over PowerPoint templates. And you will bristle to the claim that you took your colleague's parking spot. Everything from small one-on-one battles to full-blown office politics may bubble up.

Managing through interpersonal issues is an incredibly important skill. The strategies in this chapter will help you manage yourself to avoid all-out warfare, while arming you with strategies to address conflict productively and compassionately when necessary.

1) Raise Issues Thoughtfully

Bringing up issues with colleagues—whether solicited or unsolicited—is a tough nut to crack. As an employee who sincerely wants your organization to succeed, you are brave enough to raise issues that you see around you. Yet as an indispensable employee, you are smart enough to address these issues in an intelligent, constructive way.

Before blurting out your issues in anger or desperation, think carefully about the best way to address any given issue. Indispensable employees consider the following points:

- *Scope*: Whom does this issue affect? Does it affect just me, or does it affect others as well?

- *Role*: Am I the right person to be bringing up this issue? What role should I play in sorting this through?

- *Counterparty*: Whom should I address my thoughts to? Does it make sense to take this up with my manager? To the person I have a conflict with? With someone even more senior? To an anonymous committee of reviewers? The nature of the issue will help determine whom you should engage.

- *Format*: What format should I use to bring this up? Should I use a meeting, phone call, or email? (Non-face-to-face communication is rarely preferable for sensitive topics as it does not allow you to gauge your colleagues' reactions and engage around the issue.) Should I set up a new meeting to address only this issue or include it with other business? Who else should be there? What day and time of day make most sense to address it given everything else going on?

- *Delivery*: How should I present my issue? What facts or evidence do I need to have available? What is the right tone to take?

- *Potential Solutions*: How can I mitigate this issue? What solutions can I propose?

- *Personal Stake*: What part of this issue might be my responsibility? What do I have to learn from this?

In evaluating your approach against all these dimensions, remember that you are striving to be open and honest, appropriate and responsible. When you do have to deal with issues, you know there is a way to do so constructively.

—————— Indispensable Solutions ——————

- If you are feeling overwhelmed by your issue, take the time to write out an explanation of the situation, as if you were sending an email on the topic. Explain it as if you were asking someone to help resolve it. Taking the time to write it out often forces you to think through the issues and see them more clearly.

- Take responsibility. Interpersonal issues are the result of a conflict between two or more people. If something is affecting you, it is not exclusively because your ogre of a boss is imposing his will upon you; you have some part to play in the conflict as well. By simply admitting that you are contributing to a conflict and that there are things that you can do better, you help the other people in the discussion admit that there are things that they can improve upon as well.

- Remember that your colleagues and superiors want to work in a happy, healthy environment. Responsible managers want to hear about employee issues and help to address them, rather than ignore them.

- Solicited feedback—annual surveys, suggestion boxes, and 360-degree reviews—may give you a forum for airing some issues. That said, your most pressing work issues—the unpaid overtime you are working or the disrespect displayed by your VP—may not find a place in these formalized processes. Be willing to address these independently if the need arises.

- If your supervisor is actively seeking feedback from your team on an issue, it can be a good practice to appoint an ombudsman. An ombudsman is a representative of the team who solicits feedback from each person individually and compiles a collective response. This is a more anonymous process than asking each individual team member to disclose their point of view.

- That said, do not take apparent anonymity as carte blanche to attack your colleagues. Even if you are given an anonymous feedback form, there is always a chance that small sample sizes, characteristic writing styles, or unique examples will reveal your identity. Even though feedback is supposed to be anonymous, do not forget to be sensitive and diplomatic in your delivery.

2) Never Assume Intentionality

You submitted your laptop for routine maintenance, and when it was returned, your files were erased. You know that the IT support worker likely deleted them, but do you know why? Maybe it is because she needed to clear some space on the hard drive. Maybe she hit "Delete" by accident. Or maybe she really is being paid off by a colleague to sabotage your research. Guesses aside, you simply do not know her motives.

Never attribute motives to others. You are not in other people's heads. You do not have insight into their thoughts. You may easily have more or less information than they do, all of which colors your perspective and keeps you from accurately judging why they do the things they do.

Rather than making assumptions and accusing other people, allow others to tell you their side of the story. Begin by giving your colleagues the benefit of the doubt. Lead with curiosity and collect information by actively listening to what they say. By letting others speak, you build more understanding and empathy. Forming opinions with partial information is dangerous in both senses of the word partial; your opinions run the risk of being both incomplete and biased.

After listening, you can begin to state your view. When doing so, adopt language that withholds judgment. Avoid labeling other people's behaviors. Avoid making assumptions about their motives. Adopt the use of I/me/my language instead of more accusatory you/your language. Instead of saying "You never wash your laboratory supplies and are an irresponsible scientist," say "When you leave unwashed glasses in the sink, I am concerned for the health and safety of our team." Similarly, "You are a micromanager who cannot give me any real opportunities to work" turns into "When you review my work so closely, I feel disappointed that I cannot provide more leverage." Turning your statement from a judgment about them to an expression of your feelings rather than an assessment of their motivations makes sure you stay in the realm of what you know.

You can look both unintelligent and unkind when you reveal that your take on a situation is grossly underinformed, based on ugly rumors, or uncharitable toward your colleagues. Instead, listen to others' side of the story and deliver your own without judgment.

Indispensable Solutions

- Give your colleagues the benefit of the doubt. Your ingoing assumption about everyone should be that they are good people trying to do their best. It is unlikely that someone is intentionally being uncooperative, purposefully disagreeing with you, or out to get you. Unless you learn otherwise, assume that they are also working diligently with the best interests of the organization and their colleagues in mind. You are all supposed to be on the same team.

- You are the expert on you. Your colleague is the expert on her. You only know what you are thinking. She only knows what she is thinking. Avoid getting caught in the trap of believing that you know someone else better than she knows herself. Stay within your realm of expertise.

- When broaching a sensitive topic with a colleague, position yourself as clarifying instead of accusing. You can learn a lot by listening first; often, the issue will dissolve when you understand the situation more accurately. This greater understanding is not possible when you start with an accusation and force your colleagues to defend themselves.

3) Balance Directness and Diplomacy

When you speak directly, you prioritize values like openness and truth. You are clear and pointed to ensure understanding. Your words carry literal meaning. Facts and logic are the centerpiece; you let them do their work. Too direct, however, and you risk hurting other people.

When you speak diplomatically, you honor values like harmony and kindness. You soften the message to mitigate the pain. You are polite to save face and preserve everyone's dignity. Meaning is distilled from not only the words you use but the contextual clues as well. If you are too diplomatic, however, others lose the message entirely.

True mastery of this strategy comes in finding the sweet spot between the two—the place where the truth is clear but compassionate.

—————————— **Indispensable Solutions** ——————————

- One approach that bridges the direct and diplomatic divide is using open questions to investigate potential issues collaboratively. Instead of saying "Ricky should not be appointed project manager because he is a complete moron," you ask "What are the characteristics we need in a project manager?" Similarly, "That experiment will not work because of prohibitively high pH levels, you dolt" becomes "How is our experimental design affected by pH levels?" Instead of stating your contrary point directly, you set aside your perspective and explore the topic together.

- Simply acknowledging the points of others can go a long way toward maintaining a collegial atmosphere around disagreements. Phrases like "I see your point regarding . . ." and "I agree with you on . . ." help create points of connection. This also allows you to build a relationship with the other, even if you will eventually disagree with his or her conclusions. Admitting common ground is one way of being clear but kind.

- Though it may be transparent, the classic "feedback sandwich" can be effective. This approach involves sticking an unpalatable negative comment (think bologna, head cheese, or Spam) in between two more appetizing positive comments (think brioche, sourdough, or a nice warm croissant). That said, do not be limited by this formula; be inspired by it. You need not have a two-to-one positive-to-negative ratio in alternating sandwich format; you only need to remember to balance positive and negative in a way consistent with your observations.

- Whatever your strategy, if your counterparty begins to come around to your side on a debate, be gracious. Be sure to give her an "out" so that she can agree with your perspective without losing too much face.

- When it comes to hearing bad news, it often feels like our colleagues have earmuffs on. Sugarcoating a negative message often has unintended consequences; instead of softening the impact, it obscures the truth altogether. It is wise to default to directness when delivering bad news, even if it pains you.

4) Manage Your Emotions

You think about work at your desk, on your coffee breaks, and at lunch. And then, at the end of the day, you go home and spend your evenings decompressing, venting, rehashing, reconsidering, and otherwise digesting your day at work. Many of us spend more time working than pursuing our hobbies and more time with our colleagues than with our family and friends. Given how much we invest in work, it is hard for our jobs not to become emotional at some point.

While admitting that work is personal, you need to figure out how to manage your emotions professionally. Managing your emotions does not mean squelching them. Be it anger, glee, or existential angst, the emotions that work stirs up in you are all valid. You should feel and digest all of them. That said, you should also manage where and how you display those emotions. Indispensable employees rule their emotions instead of letting their emotions rule them. They consciously choose where and when they show these emotions in the workplace.

Indispensable Solutions

- You are sitting at your desk and seething about something. You cannot think of anything else. You are distracted, unproductive, and, frankly, pissed. Try this tactic to vent your frustrations: Funnel all your emotions into a strongly worded email. You probably wanted to send a strongly-worded email anyway, so write it all down. Say everything you want to say, but, importantly, do not put anyone's name in the "To" field. Instead, make yourself hit "Delete." Like your middle school journal, the writing will be cathartic; unlike your middle school journal, you do not run the risk of anyone tracking down your unfiltered thoughts.

- Do not whine. If there is a real issue to be addressed, be thoughtful and responsible about bringing it up, but do not needlessly complain. Save it until you get home and can do your kvetching outside of a work environment.

- Crying at work and getting drunk at the office holiday party have something in common: in both cases, you often end up hurrying to the bathroom. Our emotions are real and need expression; that said, when possible, it is wise to choose how, where, and to what effect to share those emotions. Even if you need to excuse yourself abruptly, it can be better to run to the bathroom than to cry in your manager's office. Alternatively, if you choose to stay in a situation in which you are crying, be aware that others may have strong reactions to your intense show of emotion.

- Even if you decide to strategically show your anger in the workplace, you should not yell. There are better ways to get things done. This is one manner of conduct that is difficult for others to forget.

EXCEED EXPECTATIONS

Managers often have a hard time describing what they do. They say their job involves organizing, leading, directing, or perhaps just managing itself. As an underling, this may seem ridiculous to you. While you slave away, you are convinced that your manager spends her time golfing, chatting up college buddies on the phone, or checking baseball scores on espn.com.

Your manager's job is legitimately hard to describe, likely because she is doing a lot of intangible thinking work. While you code one specific component of your app, she coordinates across programmers to ensure that the look and feel is consistent. While you attend to customers across your territory, she is planning the strategy to find the next million dollars of sales. In short, while you may execute a tangible task, she is required to do the critical thinking necessary to put it all together and make the system work as well as possible.

If you aspire to become indispensable, you need to do this higher-level thinking work as well. Sure, it is more taxing on the brain, but as an indispensable employee, you are willing to take on the challenge. The following strategies will help you push from executing your primary responsibilities effectively to doing more advanced, secondary thinking about your work, thereby gaining responsibility, independence, and respect.

CHAPTER TEN

Consider Your Work from Every Angle

As an employee, you have a choice: Do you operate narrowly, executing only the task at hand? Or do you take broader ownership for your piece of the puzzle?

It is simple—and almost relieving—to focus exclusively on the task at hand. It takes less thinking. It takes less energy. When things go wrong adjacent to you, you can easily claim innocence. No one can blame you for only doing what was asked of you, right?

If you said yes, you are thinking too narrowly. It is time for a mindset shift. Assuming broad ownership for your work may be the hardest change to make on the road to indispensability. You must start to see beyond the immediate task. You must consider not only the execution of your work, but its connections to potential root causes, the big picture, broader implications, and even next steps. You must see yourself more and more clearly as a piece of the organization—and take ownership beyond the narrow scope of your assignment.

But how do you expand your view? How do you see and take responsibility for aspects of your work that were previously invisible to you? One powerful way is to look at any given situation from "the four directions." Imagine yourself and your work at the center of a compass. From this vantage point, you can look up, down, left, and right (or, alternatively, north, south, east, and west). When you look in each direction, you see something different that brings your current work into perspective (see Figure 1). For example, looking up connects you to the big picture, while looking down helps you see the implications, or "so what?" of your work. Similarly, looking left (or backward) helps you dig into the root causes that lie behind your current situation while looking right (or forward) helps you look toward the next steps. Thinking in the four directions provides a prompt to look up from your immediate task and

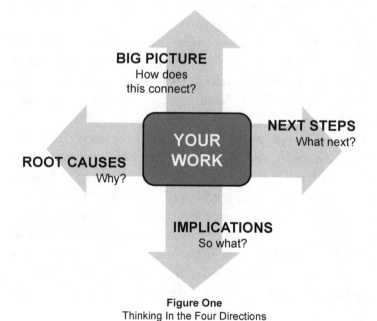

Figure One
Thinking In the Four Directions

see the relevant adjacencies. You take a broader view on your work and own everything related to it.

1) Get to the Root Causes

Moving left (or backward) is all about getting to the root causes behind your situation. This is when you imitate Sherlock Holmes. His deeply inquisitive, highly dubious approach helped him to recover incriminating photographs, solve murders, and deduce secret identities. Who else could figure out the beggar in the opium den was leading a double life? Though you need not buy yourself a basset hound and comically large magnifying glass, you should always push to uncover the real issues in every situation.

To do this, do not stop your investigation once you reach the superficial answers. When you realize that sales are down 34 percent, get curious and keep digging. Are sales down consistently across all products? Are sales down in a few specific customer accounts? If a few accounts are the cause, are these accounts managed by the same salesperson? Are they in the same region of the country? Are they served by the same distribution center?

You will know that you are at the root of a problem when the solution becomes crystal clear and highly actionable. What is the solution to sales being down 34 percent? Sell more, of course! But what, to whom, and how? This first answer does not result in any clear course of action. On the other hand, if you know that the sales decline was related to a loss of the flagship account, then you are getting somewhere. You can talk to the sales contact for the account and set up a meeting with the customer who has defected. When you understand the real issues, the path to correcting them becomes clear.

Never stop at a superficial reason, but instead put on your best detective hat and suss out the real issues at stake.

──────────── **Indispensable Solutions** ────────────

- Imitate the management gurus of Toyota. Ask yourself the one big question to diagnose what is going on: *Why?* The rule of thumb is that you should ask why at least five times to get to the root cause of an issue.

- When searching for the root causes, remember that you are not on a witch hunt; your job is not to place blame. Instead, you are looking for the issues in both people and processes. Wherever the flaw may lie, you want to find it so that the system operates appropriately.

- Go to the source. Asking the customer can be a difficult but often direct way to figure out where the issue might be.

2) See the Big Picture

Think back on those activity books you used to do as a kid: connect-the-dots, paint-by-numbers, word jumbles. Do not be a paint-by-numbers kid, someone who executes only within the bounds of what you have been given. Instead, be a connect-the-dots kid. Doing this happens in two steps: first, you see the big picture, and second, you make explicit connections between that understanding and your particular work.

Start to gain a big-picture perspective by moving above your work and putting it in context. Begin by looking for the relationships between the broader mission of your organization, your specific role within it, and this particular task. Think broadly about how everything fits together. Ask yourself: *How*

*does this task connect to the high-level goals? Why is this an import-
ant piece of the puzzle?*

While seeing the big picture more clearly is in itself helpful, the point of moving up is enabling you to perform better
on your responsibilities. As you move through your work, ask
yourself how what you are doing and learning connects with
the overall approach. See the connections, consider what you
might do about them, and raise them with your manager. This
is the real value in stepping above your work and connecting it
to the big picture.

Indispensable Solutions

- You can often track down a good articulation of the "big
  picture" in formal company documents. Look for strategic plans, formal lists of projects, or priorities to help you
  think about the whole organization from an executive's
  perspective.

- When trying to understand the big picture, it can be helpful to consider the bigger reasons behind what you have
  been asked to do. What will recutting the sales numbers
  by geography show? What impact will reformatting the
  reports have? What is the motivation for moving the meeting back three weeks? Understanding the purpose for your
  task helps make the big picture clear.

- Think through your interdependencies—the places where
  your project is reliant on other projects or departments
  in order for you to stay on track. Similarly, think of the
  interdependencies where you are the counterparty supporting someone else's progress. Bring a big-picture view
  to your interactions in both situations so that you can

support one another—and the overall organization's agenda—accordingly.

- Note the other parts of your organization that you frequently run into during the course of your work. Do you always end up in meetings with Suzuki from accounting or Maria from engineering? Reach out to those other people to find synergies or simply brainstorm how you can work better together.

3) Think Through the Implications

Thinking through implications will help you to figure out the broader impact of your work. Imagine implications as the rings that develop when you drop a pebble into a pond. Your work is the impact that breaks the surface of the water. The inner rings that appear are the immediate ramifications—how your work changes your own focus or the way you execute. Ask yourself: *What do I know now that I did not know previously? How does this change my priorities?*

Beyond that, however, there may be other, deeper levels of implications. Moving down and out, there may be concentric circles of impact—the implications for your team, your department, and the organization as a whole. How does your work impact them? What should your team and your organization do that they were not doing previously? What should they stop doing because it is no longer valuable? How should the broader allocation of time, money, and resources shift?

Thinking this way, you will be able to better see the implications for each level of those affected: yourself, your manager, your department, and your company. This is the bigger "so what?" you are seeking. This is the experience of moving down.

––––––––––––––––– **Indispensable Solutions** –––––––––––––––––

- Discovering a bigger "so what?" may call into question the company's current allocation of resources, including money, people, and management bandwidth. For example, after reforecasting your product's sales, you may realize that you do not have enough manufacturing capacity dedicated to meet your orders. Wisely point out these allocation questions without jumping too far into the fray yourself. Management will have to make the call on relative priorities, but they will be glad you brought up the question sooner versus later.

- Honing your ability to see the broader "so what?" helps develop your business judgment. While you may not be the person who makes the strategic decisions today, posing the strategic questions prompted by your "so what?" thinking gives you practice for tomorrow. Over time and with experience, you move from identifying the bigger questions and proposing possible answers to making the decisions yourself.

- Seeing the broader implications helps you anticipate the roadblocks that you may soon face. In particular, it may help you see potential internal resistance to the ideas you propose. (For more, see chapter 8, strategy 1, "Anticipate Roadblocks.")

4) Figure Out What Comes Next

"Sit, Fido, sit. Good dog. Now roll over. And beg."

However much you may envy their afternoon naps and free lunches, none of us wants to be treated like a dog. Trained to do a limited number of tricks at his master's command, a good dog merely executes what he has been told to do. He does not particularly want to roll over. He does not know when he will be asked to roll over next. And he probably does not find rolling over all that fulfilling. Let us be honest: he is in it for the bacon-flavored treats.

"Analyze. Execute. Present. Good employee." Do not wait around for your boss to give you commands. Instead of working like a dog, become your own master. When you think to the right (or forward), you consider "What's next?" From this perspective, you articulate the immediate next steps for yourself and others. You can take control of the situation by figuring out what needs to be done and proposing this to your boss.

Once you start proposing the next steps to pursue and planning your own work, you will not want to go back. Just as it can be discouraging to execute the commands of others, so it is empowering to be the one setting the path. The indispensable employee enjoys figuring out the path himself and being responsible for where his work is going. Onward and upward.

—————————— **Indispensable Solutions** ——————————

- Think through next steps before you discuss your work with your manager. Even if the next steps you propose are flawed, your hypothesis of what needs to happen will show your manager that you are thinking ahead and proactively trying to deliver more value.

- When considering next steps, you will likely come up with ideas of what other people should be doing to push the peanut as well. While you may not be able to formally assign this work to others, you can connect with them to understand what is currently being done and how your ideas might fit in. For example, while working on developing your app, you realize that a key next step is getting marketing to approve the wireframes. Figuring out who would review these, how much time it might take, and what the reviewers need from you is all useful context for figuring out next steps with your manager. To be clear, running down this information should not delay updates with your manager; it is a bonus if you have it, however.

- Make your next steps actionable. The clearer and more specific your next steps are, the more likely you are to follow through and complete them. Review chapter 6, strategy 2, "Pump Up Productivity," for tips on writing powerful to-dos.

- Though indispensable employees take the initiative to figure out what the next steps are, they are always sensitive to confirm direction with their managers before marching onward. They do not want to undermine their manager or move out of step. Flip back to chapter 5 for strategies that help you set yourself in the right direction even if you feel certain what that direction will be.

CHAPTER ELEVEN

Contribute Beyond Yourself

The indispensable employee does not stop when her job is done. Instead, she is compelled to make a greater contribution to her organization; she looks to go over and above.

So far, all the strategies of *Indispensable* have focused on helping you do the tasks related to your specific job exceptionally well. Chapter 11, however, takes a more meaningful step beyond your current role. Going over and above involves taking the initiative for something that, though not related to your job description, is on the critical path for your organization.

There are many ways to go over and above. You can stretch to do portions of your manager's job and provide better leverage. You can suggest improvements for the broader organization. You can even mentor colleagues. The following strategies will help you think through ways to provide more value for your manager, your peers, and your organization as a whole.

1) Do Your Boss's Job

Put yourself in your boss's size-ten loafers, size-eight stilettos, or size-six work boots. What are your boss's priorities? What is he or she most concerned with today? What does he or she need to do next? And most importantly, how can you support your boss in achieving the overall mandate? Putting yourself in your boss's shoes will help you to see better how you can be most useful to him or her. At the end of the day, your job is to make your boss's job easier. You do not need to walk a mile in your boss's shoes, but trying them on for a while can be a useful exercise.

Before stretching to take on parts of your manager's job, you must align with your manager. You cannot (metaphorically) steal his shoes and walk around in them. Instead, you need to ask which parts of his job you can better support, which activities you may be able to try to learn, and in which places you can be helpful. If your manager has a developmental view of the world, he should respond not by giving you his grunt work, but by carving off a couple of interesting tasks that you can try out as an apprentice to advance your skills.

──────────── **Indispensable Solutions** ────────────

- Think about how your manager engages in order to see the tangible actions you could take to be more helpful: When your manager reviews your work, what will he say? What will his questions be? And when you leave his office, what will he need to do next? Start by proposing that you take on the tasks adjacent to the work you already do.

- Keep your eyes peeled for tasks that are not part of your manager's day-to-day activities. Since he did not have these planned into his workflow, they are some of the easiest tasks to let you take the first pass on. Volunteer to draft the extra memo your manager needs to send out. Ask if you can help him think through the first presentation on a new product. Though volunteering for these types of opportunities may take time beyond your typical hours, the extra hours you spend working will be some of the most challenging, satisfying hours you spend at work.

- While walking in your boss's shoes, you will inevitably end up doing new tasks that you know little about. When you are taking on a stretch task, have a little faith in yourself. Give yourself permission to try, draw intelligently on all your resources, and do your best. Trust that your best shot at this new challenge will be defensibly decent. Your manager will be delighted to have a decent draft to start from rather than starting at the beginning himself. Regardless of your approach, suck it up and give it a shot for the sake of learning.

- Though going over and above is important to making you indispensable, remember that your primary responsibility is to your formal job. Passing on your primary job responsibilities to do incremental extras can make you look like you consider yourself too good for your current job. This will not look like overdelivering but instead like poor prioritization or overreaching. Make sure that you continue to excel at executing your current job while truly going above and beyond.

2) Evolve the System

Though filled with free snacks and comfy chairs, the corporate jet is not always the best place for a clear perspective. Due to the distance from the ground and abundant cloud cover, the jet's thirty-thousand-foot view obscures much of the reality of what is happening on the ground. From high above, the president, CEO, or Grand Poohbah of your organization gets only a bird's-eye view of the situation. When she looks down at you laboring away, she sees only a dot of a person in a slight blur of activity. While she may seem to think things are going well or poorly at any given point in time, she really is not close enough to say how or why.

Similarly, your manager, flying in a helicopter around 1,200 feet, still has a hazy view of the situation. He may know that you have been running into issues, but he cannot describe them in detail. He is similarly distant from the realities on the ground.

You, on the other hand, are on the ground, elbow-deep in the nitty-gritty reality of your work. Whatever the task, you are the person closest to the details. You know better than anyone how the system works, where there are problems, and, potentially, ways to fix them. Given your proximity and direct experience, you may well be the right person to determine how things can be done better, faster, and more effectively in your corner of the world.

Indispensable employees are interested in making their work easier and making the organization more effective by improving the system. They note ways to improve their workflow and bring them up to their managers. When given the opportunity to take on the challenge, they are excited about designing solutions and implementing them. If the ideas make sense in the bigger picture, they help to evolve the system and roll them out broadly.

—————————— **Indispensable Solutions** ——————————

- Diagnose your pain points at work: What little things do you spend a disproportionate amount of your time doing? Can you find a better way to do them? Is there an approach that frees up your time to do more interesting, more complex work?

- Think like an efficiency consultant: What processes can be systematized? What systems can be automated? Look for room to formalize and improve the way things are done.

- With your eye for detail, you will often see issues that others do not even realize existed. Take the initiative to make things better. Do not limit yourself to fixing big headline problems only; look to address the little bugs in the system before they grow into bigger beasts.

- When assessing the feasibility of your ideas for improvement, keep the big picture in mind. Your idea may make sense for you, but does it make sense when you consider the whole company? Does it set a precedent that impacts others? Does it change a process that others are dependent upon? Identify the highest-value adjustments, but also make yourself wise to the bigger ramifications of your ideas. In some situations, you will want to understand how the solution might play out at a company-wide level before committing yourself. See chapter 10, strategy 2, "See the Big Picture," for more on this.

3) Mentor to Manage

You have been at your job for a while now and you are itching to move up. Unfortunately, for whatever reason, building out your own team and managing others are not in the cards yet.

In this situation, the indispensable employee takes the initiative and volunteers herself to mentor others informally. Though mentoring peers and juniors on work that is not strictly your responsibility may seem like a waste of time, it is a terrific opportunity for you to develop your management skills. Though you may not have oversight for the work, you can share your essential learnings, coach someone through a task, or give constructive suggestions. If approached intelligently, mentoring opportunities may also turn into management opportunities when supervisors see the value you are adding.

—————————— **Indispensable Solutions** ——————————

- Make sure your mentoring is welcome. Wise employees will be excited for the guidance, while nervous ones may be set on the defensive. Only mentor those who invite your input, and never slip into playing the renegade manager role; your goal is to be helpful and additive, not to disrupt the current order of things.

- Find ways to deliver guidance to new colleagues in an inoffensive way. Often, as they are even newer at the company than you, they are unaware of internal standards and expectations. Giving context on "how it is done here" can be a good first step. For example, when showing a colleague how to format something to be company-standard, try the construction "There is no reason you should know this as it is an internal expectation, but . . ."

- Beyond the technicalities of the job, feel free to share political lessons, unspoken rules, and learnings about leadership styles with those you mentor. These are some of the hardest lessons to learn and often take a long time. Helping your colleagues read between the lines will enable the whole team perform more effectively. Most likely, your manager will know where they picked up this savvy understanding and appreciate it.

• As you start to mentor and manage others, ensure that you are willing to give credit where credit is due. Hoarding credit points to an insecurity and fundamental lack of confidence. A willingness to let your colleagues shine as talented performers shows that you are so comfortable with yourself that you can help your teammates perform at their peak as well.

4) Volunteer for the "Next Big Thing"

Your job may feel like the same thing every day. You may feel like your organization sells the same products to the same customers in the same ways. However static things look from your corner of the world, there is someone, somewhere, thinking about what comes next. It might be a new product, a new market, or an entirely new line of business, but regardless, it is coming your way. As the adage says, you and your company must "change or die" to survive in the marketplace.

This "next big thing" is some project or program designed to help your organization succeed in a competitive landscape. As such, the team tackling it will have a big, high-profile challenge in front of them. The executive team will want to put their best players on this project. Those chosen participants will get insight into what is going on more broadly with the organization and will have the chance for their work to gain unusual visibility with the executives. It is a chance to step up to the challenge.

As an indispensable employee, you want to be involved in the next big thing instead of being subject to it. Sniff out the opportunity, raise your hand to participate, and take the chance to impress.

Indispensable Solutions

- Tune your antennae in to pick up on what the next big thing might be. What are the executives talking about? What are competitors doing? What might be the source of the next great innovation? Talk to others in your organization who seem to be in the know about extraordinary projects and programs.

- Look for the intersection of a unique opportunity and your specific skill set. While it can be smart to volunteer to do whatever needs to get done (particularly at a junior level), you should not take on an optional assignment in which your chances of succeeding are low. Being stretched and challenged by the project is good; setting yourself up for failure in a high-profile situation is not.

- Think back to school; consider this an extracurricular activity. Get buy-in from your supervisor about how much of your time you should allocate to the project. Ultimately, though, be willing to invest time over and above your day job as necessary.

- The new endeavor that you are devoted to may succeed wondrously or fail completely. Secure the support of your manager that, regardless of the outcome of this project, this is a good learning opportunity for you and a chance to contribute to the organization. While you want to enjoy the upside of the project going well, make sure your reputation is not sullied if it goes poorly; with a project this big and important, it cannot be entirely your fault if there are challenges.

- Ultimately, working on the next big thing requires a degree of courage. Make a list of your fears: *I may not have enough time to do my day job, and my manager will be angry. I may love the new work and leave my current team, breaking relationships. The project may fail. I may be overloaded and not have time to work out.* Look your fears in the face and say yes to them. Saying yes to fears defuses their power and lets you see the risks more rationally, instead of getting emotionally caught up in trying to avoid them.

CHAPTER TWELVE

Drive Your Development from the Start

As an indispensable employee, you have high hopes for yourself. Instead of waiting to be plucked out of the ranks and recognized for your brilliance, you pragmatically realize that no one is as invested in your development as you. To move up from your current position, you take responsibility for your ongoing professional development.

First, you need to articulate your goals and envision what you are working toward. As you start on your journey, you look inward for honest self-assessments of your own performance, identifying how you can grow as a person. You simultaneously seek out feedback from others that helps you see yourself more clearly. Ultimately, you prove your worth to your colleagues and build a network of supporters who can testify to your ever-increasing qualifications.

Failing to push forward and develop yourself results in stagnation, disengagement, and, ultimately, dissatisfaction at work. To borrow from Zen imagery, the indispensable employee is a bubbling brook, always running, moving forward, changing, shifting, and progressing. On the other hand, without dedicating yourself to constant improvement you become a stagnant pond. Failing to flow, you slowly cover over with a layer of green slime, stinking up the surroundings. Eventually, after all the fish turn belly-up, some developer buys the property, fills in the cesspool, and builds a parking lot on top. Drive your own professional development or risk being bulldozed.

1) Articulate Your Bigger Ambitions

You will get the most out of your job if you have a broader professional plan and vision of how this role fits into your trajectory. Know what your ambitions are: What do you want? Where do you want to end up inside or outside of your organization? How does this job contribute to that goal? Your job will only be fulfilling if it dovetails with your ambitions and helps you to achieve your personal goals.

Once you have this clarity on what you want, you must pair it with the determination to try. You know that you have much to learn and many ways to improve, but you will nonetheless apply yourself to achieve your dreams. Your clarity around your ambitions and your diligence in working to achieve them work hand in hand to make you indispensable.

―――――――――― **Indispensable Solutions** ――――――――――

- Be explicit about your ambitions by committing them to writing. Write down your goals for the short term (six months to one year), for the longer term (three to five years), and for your lifetime.

- Make your ambitions clear to your manager as well. You need not disclose all the details of your twenty-year career plan, but a manager who knows what you really want is often able to see opportunities that you may not have imagined. Without knowing what you truly want, she may assume you are happy where you are and miss making a beneficial connection for you.

• Articulating your ambitions allows you to see your job in the context of your broader life goals. This helps you to prioritize the relative demands of your job versus other aspects of your life. Understanding the relative value that you put on becoming indispensable versus training for your triathlon or spending time with your two-year-old will help you to draw the line on how much effort to invest in your work.

2) Agree Upon Your Path and Progress

After figuring out the general lay of the land, you need to develop the roadmap for your professional development trajectory. Unlike driving directions that take everyone along the same fastest route, this roadmap will be personalized. You will have your own unique destination. You will choose your own combination of highways and back roads. You may even elect to take a couple of scenic routes—ways that may look circuitous to others but add to your experience of the journey.

Start by working with your manager to customize your route within the company now. Where do you want to go? What do you have to do to succeed? What roles do you want, and what promotions are you gunning for? What kinds of projects support these ambitions? Whether they formally state it or not, managers often hold a vision of what each employee needs to demonstrate to move forward. The indispensable employee makes sure that this vision does not go unarticulated, but is instead discussed, debated, and formalized in a development plan. He works with his manager to establish a clear, commonly understood set of goals. This helps him to focus his efforts on the most important issues, rather than trying to tackle every job responsibility at once. It also gives him a reference against which to check his progress and ensure he stays the course.

Agree on where you are going, make sure your manager is along for the ride, and set the right checkpoints along the way.

Indispensable Solutions

- Schedule an initial meeting with your manager with the purpose of establishing your professional development plan. Managers are typically receptive to requests to understand what you want and to talk you through what you might do to become a better member of the team. Do not wait for the annual review cycle to come around or for someone to give you a standard review form.

- Take it upon yourself to understand the processes for promotions, job changes, and special projects at your company. How do they work? How are people selected? When do they happen? Who makes the decisions?

- Understand the various levels of performance on a granular level. What does average performance look like? What constitutes exceptional performance?

- Having clear parameters helps you avoid getting stuck in a trap of favoritism. Even if your manager may simply get along with someone else better (they are always having lunch and going out for karaoke together!), she will not be able to deny your performance against the criteria that you jointly set. Use those previously discussed criteria as a touchpoint for your developmental conversations around where you are headed and how far away you are from your goals.

- Do not let formal credentials stand in your way. Be aware of what qualifications or credentials you need to advance, and proactively sign yourself up for the classes or programs required.

- Having a plan from the outset allows you to check back against that initial vision. Where have you gone right? Where have you gone wrong? What skills do you have to prove you possess to move to the next level? Check back in with yourself every one to two weeks and with your manager about every month.

- To the extent that you can, try to participate in projects that give you opportunities to prove yourself and to practice the specific skills on your development plan. If you need to show your financial prowess, ask to review the budgets. If you are practicing your presentation skills, volunteer to train more junior employees. Do not wait until the perfect project falls in your lap; actively pursue opportunities to give yourself the experience you need even if they are a bit beyond your formal job responsibilities.

- One of your manager's responsibilities is writing your performance review. Putting everything in one place that your manager can easily reference will help ensure you get credit for all your good work. Start by combing through your work and providing a synopsis of your performance that she can use as a starting point. Make sure to include both responsibilities and results (quantified if possible). Follow the format of your HR system to make it easy for your manager to use. When done well, this summary will help her to assess accurately where you are along your path and write you a review that will feel both accurate and developmentally helpful.

3) Cultivate Self-Awareness

You are your own worst critic; you can be the harshest judge around. Similarly, though, you are your own best critic; your self-assessments are often the most insightful and meaningful. If honest with yourself, you are able to see an internal level of depth that is obscured to others. Therefore, in addition to running down feedback from others, cultivate your own self-awareness.

Begin by reflecting on how your words and actions appear to others, be they your superiors, your peers, or your juniors. Try to step outside of yourself. Do you come off as an overly confident show-off? As a wilting wallflower? As an expert on one particular subject? As a broad jack-of-all-trades? What is your overall brand, and what does that tell you about yourself?

A second way to build self-knowledge is to consider your unique constellation of strengths and weaknesses. What are your unique strengths? Which of those seem to come naturally? Which have you intentionally developed over time? What are your particular weaknesses? Which get in your way? Which have you learned to manage or mitigate?

Finally, step back from your situation. Look for the self-knowledge that resides in your intuition instead of in your intellect. What are you missing? What does your gut know that your head does not yet understand? If you were less invested in feeling happy or looking good, what might you see about yourself?

These are only a handful of ways to begin to cultivate self-awareness. Using these approaches or others, indispensable employees seek to know themselves and use this information wisely.

Indispensable Solutions

- Each organization seems to have its own favorite selection of assessments; take advantage of what is offered and seek out others if none are available. The Myers–Briggs Type Indicator (MBTI) and Gallup's Clifton Strengths assessment are two perennially popular options, but any assessment that prompts you to think critically about yourself is useful in pushing your development. Entertain the possibility that the assessments could be accurate and use them as a prompt for deeper reflection.

- Be aware of your own limitations and be willing to ask for help when you need it. Similarly, be aware of the places where you have distinctive strengths, and know your worth. The most successful employees often start by executing remarkably in their "power alley" and slowly building out their ability to deliver on a broader and broader set of tasks.

- Keep track of your learnings as you come across them. You should track both what you are learning through feedback at work and also what you are learning as a person. This tracking enables you to review lessons, keep an up-to-date résumé, and, perhaps most importantly, accelerate your learning in the future. Your journal is a convenient location to keep these insights.

4) Run Down the Feedback You Need

One of the most common complaints about work is that employees do not receive enough feedback. They think they are doing the right thing in the right way for the right reasons, but they have not received substantive confirmation of that from their managers. They slide by without serious encouragement or discouragement, finally inferring "I must be doing okay as no one has said anything, and I have not been fired yet." Needless to say, this situation does not maximize development and growth.

Indispensable employees do not wait around for the feedback that may never come. As with most situations in the workplace, they take responsibility for the issue. They proactively run down the feedback they need.

Seeking out feedback can be both a formal and an informal process. Formally, your organization may have an annual or semiannual review system in which all employees are involved. Take advantage of this system, participate fully, and take the feedback to heart. You can go beyond this formal feedback, however; and, as you guessed, indispensable employees always do. Indispensable employees ask their managers for immediate informal feedback on the spot. They also set up feedback-oriented meetings periodically to solicit more direct feedback. By making it indisputably clear that they are sincerely invested in improving themselves, they give their managers freedom to give the feedback they need.

─────────── Indispensable Solutions ───────────

- Remember that feedback is a mechanism through which you understand what to change and start to move forward. By continuing to do what you did yesterday, last week, and last month, you will inevitably stay where you have been. Only by figuring out the next challenge and pursuing it enthusiastically will you move forward.

- Seek out feedback from all sources. The indispensable employee takes lessons from many people, not just from their superiors. They are interested in what everyone—from managers to peers to juniors—has to share with them and see value in multiple perspectives.

- That said, evaluate the source of the feedback. Does the giver have enough information to provide a sound critique of your performance? Is he likely to be biased? Though infrequent, there are times when you should temper your acceptance of feedback based on the profile of the giver. Otherwise, keep an open mind to the thoughts that others have so generously shared with you.

- Having completed an assignment, ask for informal feedback immediately. As impressions will be freshest at this time, this feedback is often easier for your manager to give and more useful for you. Simple questions like "Is this what you expected?" "How would you have done this differently?" and "What can I do better next time?" help prompt your manager to give brief, targeted feedback on the spot.

- For big events like presentations or conference calls, mention to your colleagues in advance that you will want feedback on the work to follow. As they are primed to provide it, the quality of their feedback will increase by an order of magnitude. Note that, since this requires a fair investment of attention and energy on their side, you should use this only periodically on major assignments.

- Giving quality feedback takes time and thought. Given this, it is possible to ask for feedback too frequently and become a drain on your manager. Be clear that you are always open to hear feedback, but focus your specific asks for feedback on the situations most useful to you (e.g., the first time you present, on a piece of work that will be often repeated, or in a situation where the feedback may be applied to analogous situations).

- When trying to understand the source of criticism, ask for your manager to give you examples to clarify the feedback for you. Though you want to avoid sounding defensive, you sincerely want to understand what triggered the feedback. Never go about explaining to her why you did such and such and therefore why the feedback is wrong.

- Make sure that criticism translates into clear, constructive mandates for the future. Ask "So instead of X, I should do Y next time?" The feedback you receive should result in tangible actions for tomorrow in the office rather than generic mandates to do better next time.

- In addition to informal, in-the-moment feedback, set quarterly check-ins to solicit feedback and share how you are feeling about your performance and role. Do not let your annual performance review be a surprise.

- You have a right to receive feedback in your job. Unfortunately, you only retain this right if you act upon the feedback given. Failing to react to feedback, particularly after asking your manager to invest her time to think closely about your development, implies that while you care enough to ask her to invest in you, you cannot be bothered to invest in yourself. If you fail to implement feedback enough times, you will lose your right to it.

- Do not take feedback too hard. Negative feedback does not mean that you are a bad person, that you are horrible at your job, or that you will never amount to a hill of beans in the working world. Yes, it means that you have something to work on, but do not let it destroy your confidence.

- When receiving positive feedback, receive it graciously and confidently. Do not deflect the compliment. A simple "Thank you" is appropriate.

- Keep track of your own trajectory. Keep a record—a Word file, a work journal, or a note on your phone—of all your professional development goals. Use this file to record suggestions generic to succeeding in your job and feedback specific to you. Reviewing this reference from time to time will help you recall all the things on which you should be working.

5) Build a Network of Supporters

As you work with more and more people within your organization, you will have the opportunity to create a community of promoters or a community of detractors. It is up to you: Will you build a cheering section or a peanut gallery?

The members of your cheering section are the people at work who stick up for you. As your superiors, they champion you for new projects, support your case in promotion decisions, monitor your professional development, and invest in your career progression. As your juniors, they come to you for advice, seek out working with you, and ask you to join them for Taco Tuesday. Regardless of position, though, your cheerleaders stick up for you. This is not to say that they have an overly rosy picture of who you are; they simply embrace you and believe in your potential. They want to see you thrive in your organization. They love working with you, for you, or simply near you. In fact, they just like work better because you are there. While you stop short of outfitting them all in pleated skirts and pom-poms, you know that they cheer you on in any situation.

But beware the opposite; you do not want to create a peanut gallery. The peanut gallery watches your every move, sniggering at any misstep and lobbing down disparaging remarks at every opportunity. They are a whole contingent of those detractors, yelling from the balcony and impeding your progress. Composed of individuals of all tenures and job descriptions, the peanut gallery does not particularly like you. Frankly, they would rather see you leave than stay and succeed.

Though these classifications will not be so dramatic in the real world, they are still apt. Cultivate your enthusiastic cheerleaders and avoid creating detractors.

Indispensable Solutions

- Though your manager is doubtless your most important promoter, everyone is a potential cheerleader. The new intern you mentored over the summer can sing your praises for showing him the ropes. The finance team can respect you for turning in prompt and honest expense reports. And the administrative assistant whom everyone else ignores can become a fan of your restraint from picking all the red M&M's out of his candy jar.

- While you want to cultivate a broad network of supporters, there is often only room for a handful of deep, committed mentor relationships. Be thoughtful about whom you hope to learn from over the long-term. These relationships will often grow organically, though you may benefit, later down the line, from making them more explicit.

- Mentors can become some of your most important cheerleaders, but beware of overstepping the bounds of these relationships. A mentor invests her own time and energy in your development—and often for little more than a thank-you. Do not abuse your relationship by taking up too much of her time. Instead, use your mentor's time respectfully, discussing well-chosen topics and offering up well-considered questions. Be as responsible with your mentor's time as you would be with your manager's.

- Include your cheerleaders in your decision-making processes. Check in with them at major decision points as well as periodically to keep in touch. Not only will they have good advice for the current turning point, but they will also feel more committed when you come back to them at the next juncture.

CONCLUSION

Though you have reached the end of *Indispensable*, your journey to becoming an indispensable employee is just beginning.

While each job has its own keys to success, the strategies of *Indispensable* will help you get started off right. Pick and choose which among them are most useful for you in your current work situation; perhaps chapters 2 and 4 are most relevant for one project whereas chapter 3 is most relevant for another. Regardless, take the strategies laid out in *Indispensable* to heart. Whatever combination of approaches works best, continue to implement them in this job and jobs to come.

Over time, many of the indispensable strategies will become second nature to you. Was there any other way to prepare for meetings effectively? Was there any other approach to communicating your work to your supervisor? The *Indispensable* approach will, with sincere effort and thoughtful application to your situation, become your own. Furthermore, as you grow, you will find yourself tweaking the indispensable strategies to make them even more compatible with your role and personality.

Over time, as applying the indispensable strategies becomes increasingly routine for you, you will find yourself expecting a similarly high level of performance from others. You will want your teammates to be as effective at work as you are. Thus, you will want to share the insights of *Indispensable* with others in your organization so that they too can improve and the whole team can develop. Happily, you can be confident that applying the indispensable strategies is not a zero-sum game; when your peers learn the indispensable strategies, you benefit as well. Your interactions with them—the endless parade of meetings, conference calls, and department updates that you dreaded—become easier. You and your colleagues increasingly build a common set of expectations around how you work together. And over time, the whole organization starts to function more effectively and efficiently, making your life at work that much easier.

As you move further into your career, you will find that there are few better foundations for becoming an excellent manager than being an indispensable employee. You know what excellence looks like and set a high bar for your team. You are able to give your teammates direction to reach that aspirational target. And you remember being there yourself, so you can act with greater empathy and compassion. You were given an inside track to workplace success, and part of your excellence as an emerging manager is sharing that with your team.

But ultimately, all this work to become indispensable comes back to you. Indispensable employees know that the workplace is simply an arena for their own development as people. They measure their worth not by how indispensable their organizations judge them to be but by how fully they live out the full potential of who they truly are.

Your journey to indispensability continues from this point; may it be challenging, fulfilling, and, ultimately, worthwhile.

ACKNOWLEDGMENTS

I'm grateful for everyone who helped me develop and deliver *Indispensable*. Besides the formal interviews and surveys, this book is the result of hours of dinner table conversations with my talented friends and colleagues. I am grateful for all the conversations we shared, though I specifically want to thank the following people for their over-and-above contributions:

To my wife, Liz Callahan: Who knew that when I married you, I would not only be marrying my life partner and co-parent, but I would also be marrying the world's best grammarian and social marketing strategist? You have many talents and have brought them all to bear on this manuscript, both directly and through your support of my work. This would not have been possible without you. I hope I can return the favor and be as useful to you in your future endeavors, my love.

To my parents, David and Janice Whipple: Long ago and far away, I spent the summer in Port Huron with you. I did three things during that happy time: trained for a triathlon, cooked big dinners, and wrote this manuscript. I am grateful that those times together have translated into these pages.

To my daughter, Elliott Claire: I picked this manuscript back up and decided to make publication a reality while you slept on my lap. You were not yet a year old at the time, but you gave me the motivation to do things that I had previously perceived to be too big and left undone. You continue to challenge me to be my bigger, better self.

To Teresa Cowherd: Your continuing interest in the *Indispensable* manuscript (even years after the initial draft was complete) prompted me to pick this back up and rework the content. Thank you for providing that spark.

To Mike McKay: You taught me what fierce, unwavering sponsorship looks like. You continue to challenge me to be my best self at work and beyond. Thank you for all your support over the years—in my work, in my writing, and beyond.

To Tamar DorNer: You delivered my first half dozen or so performance reviews and, with them, so much wisdom. When we are lucky enough to connect, I still find your advice invaluable.

To Mark Horwitch: You taught me so much about the importance of being one's self in the workplace. This learning - more than anything else - fueled the revisions between the first manuscript and this final product. Thank you for bringing authenticity into my life in a bigger way.

To my friends at Bain & Company: There are so many people who have passed through Bain's halls who have mentored and coached me. I am always grateful for my years there. I look forward to seeing what remarkable things Bain continues to do.

To Stuart Friedman: You championed me until the day I turned in the manuscript – and beyond. Thank you for not only working so hard to make sure this was possible, but also for applying your critical eye to every word.

To Rebecca Strauss: Thank you for initially championing *Indispensable* (under the former, unadvisable title *Don't Get Drunk at the Holiday Party, and Twelve More Important Rules for Becoming a Rockstar Employee*). You gave me faith that this could be real someday.

To Eleanore Douglas: Ever since we were roommates long ago, I have been impressed by your intelligence and diligence. You worked hard to understand what I was trying to accomplish with this book and pushed me to think about *Indispensable* from an unfamiliar perspective. I will always value your opinion immensely.

To Katy Ganguli: Thank you for contributing your wisdom to this work. I felt both validated and challenged by getting your sharp MBA perspective. You helped to broaden and deepen *Indispensable*.

To Jes Wolfe: You helped me to push this over the line. Thank you for bringing your tech perspective to remind me, in no uncertain terms, when it was time to ship.

To Dan Whipple, Kim Fabbri, and KC George: You are my marketing consultants. Thank you for helping sort through titles and covers to make *Indispensable* stand out.

To my friends at Quill and Inkshares: I am grateful for the opportunity to publish with you. Thank you for making this a reality.

To each of my Grand Patrons: You supported the publication of *Indispensable* at the highest level, pledging your faith through preordering multiple copies of my book. You were willing to take a chance on a first-time author writing a book you had not yet read—and then to wait out an extended timeline to see what came of your bet. Without you, *Indispensable* would not exist. Thank you for your faith and your generosity.

GRAND PATRONS

Shivani Amar
Melissa Artabane
Ed Batista
Paayal Desai
Sarah Dickens
Eleanore Douglas
Kate Callahan Eilers
Jessica England
Alli Folk
Christoph Frehsee
John Garvin
KC George
Michael Gramkow
Anne Hamersky
Daniel Haspel
Paige Henchen
Katie Jenkins
Stevens Kelly
Timothy Kleiman
Zachary Levine
Marissa Limsiaco

Romy Leunig
JoAnn Lynen
Mark Matera
Matthew Matera
The McNally Family
Aleksandra Peters
Tiffany Rech
William Shen
Carrie Simonds
Andrea Sparrey
Casey Taylor
Jade Tjia
Lauren Tulp
Beth and Michael Wagner
David and Janice Whipple
Christopher Bruce White
Michael Woodbury

INKSHARES

INKSHARES is a reader-driven publisher and producer based in Oakland, California. Our books are selected not by a group of editors, but by readers worldwide.

While we've published books by established writers like *Big Fish* author Daniel Wallace and *Star Wars: Rogue One* scribe Gary Whitta, our aim remains surfacing and developing the new author voices of tomorrow.

Previously unknown Inkshares authors have received starred reviews and been featured in the *New York Times*. Their books are on the front tables of Barnes & Noble and hundreds of independents nationwide, and many have been licensed by publishers in other major markets. They are also being adapted by Oscar-winning screenwriters at the biggest studios and networks.

Interested in making your own story a reality? Visit Inkshares.com to start your own project or find other great books.

CPSIA information can be obtained
at www.ICGtesting.com
Printed in the USA
FSHW02n2019270618
49796FS